Cambridge Elements

Elements in Politics and Society in Southeast Asia
edited by
Edward Aspinall
Australian National University
Meredith L. Weiss
University at Albany, SUNY

POLITICS IN A PANDEMIC

*Governance and Crisis Management
in Southeast Asia*

Meredith L. Weiss
University at Albany, SUNY

Shaftesbury Road, Cambridge CB2 8EA, United Kingdom

One Liberty Plaza, 20th Floor, New York, NY 10006, USA

477 Williamstown Road, Port Melbourne, VIC 3207, Australia

314–321, 3rd Floor, Plot 3, Splendor Forum, Jasola District Centre, New Delhi – 110025, India

103 Penang Road, #05–06/07, Visioncrest Commercial, Singapore 238467

Cambridge University Press is part of Cambridge University Press & Assessment, a department of the University of Cambridge.

We share the University's mission to contribute to society through the pursuit of education, learning and research at the highest international levels of excellence.

www.cambridge.org
Information on this title: www.cambridge.org/9781009479318

DOI: 10.1017/9781108933155

© Meredith L. Weiss 2025

This publication is in copyright. Subject to statutory exception and to the provisions of relevant collective licensing agreements, no reproduction of any part may take place without the written permission of Cambridge University Press & Assessment.

When citing this work, please include a reference to the DOI 10.1017/9781108933155

First published 2025

A catalogue record for this publication is available from the British Library

ISBN 978-1-009-47931-8 Hardback
ISBN 978-1-108-92778-9 Paperback
ISSN 2515-2998 (online)
ISSN 2515-298X (print)

Cambridge University Press & Assessment has no responsibility for the persistence or accuracy of URLs for external or third-party internet websites referred to in this publication and does not guarantee that any content on such websites is, or will remain, accurate or appropriate.

For EU product safety concerns, contact us at Calle de José Abascal, 56, 1°, 28003 Madrid, Spain, or email eugpsr@cambridge.org

Politics in a Pandemic

Governance and Crisis Management in Southeast Asia

Elements in Politics and Society in Southeast Asia

DOI: 10.1017/9781108933155
First published online: December 2025

Meredith L. Weiss
University at Albany, SUNY

Author for correspondence: Meredith L. Weiss, merweiss@gmail.com

Abstract: The COVID-19 pandemic offers unique insight into how regimes govern in "hard times." In Southeast Asia, public health and economic strain revealed the scope for adaptation in the face of crisis, against the pull of path-dependent habits and patterns. Recent experience of SARS and other outbreaks, as well as wider political and economic contexts, shaped readiness and responses. Especially important were legacies of the developmental-state model. Even largely absent a prior welfarist turn, core developmentalist attributes helped foster citizen buy-in and compliance: how efficiently and well states could coordinate provision of necessary infrastructure, spur biomedical innovation, marshal resources, tamp down political pressure, and constrain rent-seeking, all while maintaining popular trust. Also salient to pandemic governance were the actual distribution of authority, beyond what institutional structures imply, and the extent to which state–society relations, including habits of coercion or rent-seeking, encourage more or less programmatic or confidence-building frames and approaches.

Keywords: COVID-19, Southeast Asia, developmental state, securitization, state–society relations

© Meredith L. Weiss 2025

ISBNs: 9781009479318 (HB), 9781108927789 (PB), 9781108933155 (OC)
ISSNs: 2515-2998 (online), 2515-298X (print)

Contents

1 Introduction — 1

2 Understanding COVID-19 in Southeast Asia — 5

3 What Shaped Southeast Asian States' Performance — 13

4 Implications and Conclusions — 51

References — 69

1 Introduction

Among the most devastating and disruptive pandemics of the modern era, COVID-19 put all governments to the test. Global case-counts are in the hundreds of millions; millions have died. Even once vaccines, including lower-cost and effective alternatives, emerged, access to them remained uneven.[1] The economic implications have also been enormous, amid the abrupt, sustained cessation of cross-border flows of people – workers, tourists, students, missionaries, diplomats – alongside necessarily draconian measures to curb social interactions to inhibit spread. Such measures devastated the full range of service industries, interrupted education at all levels, impeded plantings and harvests, and scrambled production and distribution chains. By April 2020, still anticipating that the pandemic would lift by mid-year, the IMF already predicted the recessionary impact of the "Great Lockdown" to be second only to that of the Great Depression (Gopinath 2020). Indeed, economic dislocation proved both persistent and devastating – and the virus continues to circulate, with periodic surges.

Southeast Asia represents the best and the worst of pandemic response – including wide swings within the same country over time. Singapore, for instance, seemingly offered the world a masterclass of how to handle the COVID-19 pandemic, only to experience a rash of cases among its massive migrant-worker population; Thailand and Vietnam impressed observers for their apparent resistance to the virus through 2020, only to stumble in 2021 as variants proliferated and vaccination drives stalled. The Lowy Institute's Covid Performance Index positioned the Asia-Pacific region as the world's best-performing in terms of COVID-19 cases, deaths, and tests as of March 2021, but noted significant outliers, including Indonesia and the Philippines.[2] Four Southeast Asian countries – Singapore, Vietnam, Thailand, and Malaysia – also spent time in the top 20 in Bloomberg's Covid Resilience Ranking, a measure of countries' efficiency in handling the pandemic while minimizing economic disruption, though a new wave of cases in the second quarter of 2021 swept all but Singapore from those ranks.[3] All told, though, at least though early 2021, East and Southeast Asia seemed to have "weathered the economic shock and [to be] on track to do better than any other region" (Tiberghien 2021, 3).

The scale and severity of the challenge revealed wide variation in qualities of governing regimes and in state capacities and responsiveness. Singapore, Thailand, and Vietnam garnered praise as "models of effective communication

---

[1] See the WHO Coronavirus (COVID-19) Dashboard at https://covid19.who.int/ for current data.
[2] See https://interactives.lowyinstitute.org/features/covid-performance/.
[3] See https://www.bloomberg.com/graphics/covid-resilience-ranking/.

and transparency" (Djalante et al. 2020, 10), even as Indonesia and the Philippines "sent mixed and confusing messages, peddled quackery, and were largely in denial" (Abuza and Welsh 2020). However governments responded, the pandemic provided them the opportunity to assume new political powers and to intervene in the daily lives of citizens and economic affairs in ways unprecedented outside wartime. Illiberalism gained ground, but with differing character and implications. Diverse responses to common threats offer an opportunity to probe governance in the region and what accounts for disparities across cases: how governments handle crisis, who and what they prioritize, and what factors best explain these patterns. Such a review is useful for understanding the pandemic's sociopolitical hangovers, but also given the near-certainty of future crises. This inquiry aligns, too, with efforts to deploy the study of contagion to test and develop a host of social-scientific theories, on everything from state–society relations to social trust and prejudice (Singh 2024).

Scholarly work comparing responses to COVID-19 across the region has tended toward one of three approaches: institutional, policy-oriented (though at heart, also structural), or cultural. The first has dominated, especially evaluating the extent to which the pandemic accelerated democratic backsliding in the region and the implications for how states mobilized resources in response. More policy-focused work has homed in especially on the extent to which the region's quick response built on lessons learned and systems developed in the Severe Acute Respiratory Syndrome (SARS) epidemic in 2003. A third body of work has offered cultural explanations that emphasize "Asian values" of collectivism, sacrifice, and deference to authority as keys to controlling the pandemic. These approaches, examined in more depth below, offer real value, yet are incomplete: they miss a deeper institutional *and* political-cultural foundation. This study instead illuminates contemporary realities by grounding the region's experience of a twenty-first century pandemic in political-economic transformations of the 1980s–1990s.

Specifically, I argue that what the pandemic reveals is powerful institutional path-dependency, reflecting the legacy not only of experience with SARS but also of wider political and economic transformations, in three dimensions. First is the bequest of the developmental statehood, or aspirations thereto, that defined earlier postcolonial economic strategies across most of the region. In brief, this legacy appears in the political economy: the efficiency and adequacy with which states could coordinate infrastructure and innovation, marshal resources, constrain both rent-seeking and electoral pressure, and command sufficient popular trust to be confident of citizen compliance. Developmentalist history does not correlate perfectly with effective pandemic-wrangling, but it offers a useful parallel. It may be that those states well-suited for a developmental-state approach were and are those with relevant capacities – that a developmentalist legacy is an indicator for underlying attributes newly relevant now. Most important in this vein are the extent to which authority is concentrated, the balance between programmatic provision versus rent-seeking, and the extent of citizens' voluntary compliance with state directives. These qualities foreground the second dimension, the distribution of authority, which only sometimes reflects developmentalist patterns. What matters here is not simply decentralization but how central and local have come to share power and coordinate. Third, patterns of state–society relations, including hangovers from past rent-seeking or simmering illiberalism, may also diminish citizens' confidence in government directives – with potential even to unravel more helpful developmentalist or other legacies. In such cases, states might choose or be obliged to rely on a security-centered rather than more "democratic" public-health approach.

Situating Pandemic Responses

"Hard times" reveal the workings of power in ways "normal politics" cannot, laying bare the underlying bones of bodies politic. Explains Peter Gourevitch (1986, 17), reflecting on the economic shocks of the late 1970s and early 1980s, it is in such times that the "comfortable illusion" of regularized, stable systems "disintegrates," even in the liberal democracies he analyses. "Patterns unravel," he explains, "economic models come into conflict, and policy prescriptions diverge." Politics determines which choices governments take when autopilot fails (19). Meanwhile, political opportunity structures shift amid contests for attention and precedence, as state goals collide (e.g., public-health, economic, and social objectives), politicians and agencies promote policy fixes, and communities strategize, either for policy influence and resources or "to shield society from state initiatives" (Boudreau 1996, 176).

A pandemic offers a particularly apt lens on states and their leanings. A virus is oblivious to borders – and earlier efforts to combat HIV/AIDS, in particular, "embedded cosmopolitan ideas of transnational disease dynamics, requiring collective, global efforts" (Wenham et al. 2023, 435). Even so, as Evan Lieberman (2009, 2) describes of that pandemic, evidence of HIV's global spread notwithstanding, "many government leaders and citizens around the world clung to the idea that geographic, social, and political boundaries would insulate them from the contagion." Boundaries were no less salient to COVID-19: states defined the global pandemic in national terms, walling themselves in and others out, and prioritizing their own access to medical countermeasures. States, too, denounced migrants, the urban poor, or other population segments as especially suspect. Such practices amplified the threats to different categories of rights the pandemic posed – political, civil, economic, social – and focused those threats disproportionately on certain groups. (In driving its targets underground, such stigmatization is, of course, especially counterproductive to public-health efforts.) And, notwithstanding a degree of convergence in toolkits and regional institution-building and coordination (Davies 2019; Tiberghien 2021), states not only dwarfed nongovernmental and supra-state actors in authority but also responded in notably diverse ways, beyond what epidemiological indicators alone might explain (e.g. Lieberman 2009, 4–7; Wenham et al. 2023, 437–438).

This examination thus aims to situate the exceptional period of the pandemic within a longer view of state–society relations in Southeast Asia. How states in the region approached postcolonial governing challenges in decades past continues to mold state actions and societal reactions. The shock of crisis galvanizes and spotlights how present-day strains reactivate those legacies. All told, features associated with developmentalism proved especially helpful in allowing policymakers to adjudicate among conflicting priorities and reassure local communities that the sacrifices they were asked to make were warranted. Specifically, a legacy of state coordination, following decisions insulated from political and rent-seeking pressure, enacted in an environment of public trust in such decisions, allowed efficient, effective action. However, both how authority is distributed in practice and how states framed the crisis tempered straightforward translation. What matters, then, is not only the structural constraints states face as a crisis takes hold but also the space for innovation, agency, and popular acquiescence public officials can expect as they chart their response.

Clearly, even fully realized, developmentalist logic is not fully sufficient or necessarily ideal for addressing COVID-19 (or, for that matter, other global challenges, such as climate change). On the one hand, norms and citizens' expectations have changed since the developmentalist heydays of the 1970s–1990s, particularly over appropriate priorities and the relative importance of democratic qualities such as accountability and transparency. Indeed, the extent of agreement on economic performance as paramount objective was arguably overstated even then, let alone as East Asian developmental states have embraced more social-welfarist goals (Evans 2014). On the other hand, and yet more problematically, the nature of the challenges now at issue may demand tweaks to the framework. The ideal-typical developmental state is highly centralizing, allowing for national-level coordination, but constraining potentially productive subnational innovation and nimble adaptation. Moreover, an effective approach cannot focus too adamantly at the level of the nation-state.

A virus, like global warming, is inherently transnational. Permeable borders mean states focus only on citizens at their peril. Whether populations that trusted state planners amid rapid postcolonial growth, but now confront deeper inequality and reduced social mobility, remain so primed for consensual cooperation is also uncertain. But taking these caveats into account: states that temper top-down technocratic decision-making with space for local-level innovation, regional coordination, transparency, and efforts to stress cooperation and buy-in may prove not only the value of "democratic" methods for crisis-management but also the real staying power of an updated developmental statehood.

To build its case, this study capitalizes on the constrained variation among a set of Southeast Asian states – Indonesia, Malaysia, the Philippines, and Singapore – drawing secondarily on the experience especially of Thailand and Vietnam. These four primary cases have not only diversely democratic or hybrid regimes but also differing past histories of developmentalist orientations. All, too, experienced SARS in the 2000s – an important backdrop. To begin, a brief review of the course of COVID-19 in Southeast Asia clarifies why this region is such an important one to study for understanding crisis governance. With that empirical grounding, the discussion then turns to prevailing explanatory frameworks, not just for how the pandemic developed and states responded but also for what those patterns reveal about state–society relations. I next delve into, first, what seems most relevant in a developmentalist legacy to pandemic-response and how these legacies came into play; then how, and how well, center and local collaborated, with what effects; then the extent to which states could and did opt for an all-pulling-together public-health approach or defaulted to more coercive securitization. The volume concludes by considering the implications of these "hard times" for the region's states, as well as for how we study and assess them, moving forward. This analysis aims not to present a definitive last word on crisis governance but to provide an evidence-backed attempt to understand better not just how governance happens but of the conditions under which it does or should change, to be up to the task of addressing contemporary challenges.

2 Understanding COVID-19 in Southeast Asia

There is no single story of COVID-19 in Southeast Asia. Even within countries, stark differences are apparent over time[4] and across communities. In some countries, the pandemic rapidly took hold; other states were able to

---

[4] The ANU's "COVID-19 and Government Policy Response in Asia" site, https://ausnatuni.maps.arcgis.com/apps/MapSeries/index.html?appid=aca8fb4fc77743f58c2e27673828455a, presents interactive maps of the pandemic's progress and of government stress and policy responses over time.

keep it at bay at least until late-breaking variants laid siege. Singapore's story, for instance, is both of a "pandemic of inequality," evidenced by an outbreak among low-waged foreign workers in tightly packed dormitories far worse than what "the community" experienced (Y. Tan 2020), as well as of near-containment until new variants sped faster than vaccines could interdict them in mid-2021 (Lopes 2021). Experience of the pandemic proved also gendered and generation-specific. Plan International (2021) reported, for example, that school-aged girls in the region were especially negatively affected: stay-at-home orders meant their taking on more duties in the household instead of completing their studies, while boys had better access to gadgets and internet connectivity for remote learning.

Moreover, Southeast Asia's decades-long urban-development focus proved a liability. The region's megacities suffered disproportionately from lockdowns. Not only is social distancing hardly possible in crowded urban and peri-urban environments, but also, controlling movement entails limiting access to income from employment, and, hence, food and other necessities for the most vulnerable. Informal workers and migrant or undocumented populations were especially hard-hit, being so often lacking in access to welfare services or other social support (McQuay et al. 2020). Rural populations are better able to maintain social distance and tend to be less cash-dependent, and agriculture faced less disruption than other economic sectors. However, rural areas felt the strain of unprecedented urban–rural migration – for instance, among tourism-industry workers obliged to await a revival. The agricultural sector could not readily absorb such an influx, even of those with requisite skills (Pajai 2021).

It is these uneven experiences of COVID-19 within and across Southeast Asia that make this region such an important one to study for understanding crisis governance, understood as minimizing both pandemic spread and attendant socioeconomic disruption. Leveraging region-wide variation allows identification of overarching factors that shape pandemic responses and reveal underlying contours of state–society relations. (Table 1 illustrates that range, as of when vaccination was gaining ground and case-rates were at a lull, pre-Delta variant.) These factors connect seemingly disparate coronavirus subplots to trace a storyline along which one might situate Southeast Asia's comparative successes and shortcomings. This study is not the first to extract such narratives; it benefits from earlier efforts it connects and extends. Particularly salient and prevalent have been accounts that foreground *politics*, *policy*, and *culture* as key factors shaping the region's uneven responses to the pandemic. However, while each of these accounts offers real analytical utility, each also suffers from blind spots.

Table 1 COVID-19 tests, cases, and deaths, as of mid-June 2021*

	Singapore*	Thailand	Vietnam	Indonesia	Philippines	Malaysia
Cases per million pop.	10.65	47.15	112	7,018	12,065	20,468
Total cases	62,301	199,264	10,881	1,920,000	1,320,000	662,457
Deaths per million pop.	5.81	21	0.61	194.19	208.48	122.6
Total deaths	34	1,466	59	53,116	22,845	3,968
Case fatality rate	0.06%	0.74%	0.54%	2.77%	1.73%	0.6%
Tests per 1,000	2189.47	106.1	48.97	44.38	120.8	412.8
Fully vaccinated	32.28%	2.37%	0.06%	4.25%	1.72%	4.37%

* Most data are from 14 June 2021; some counts range from 7 to 15 June. Dubious testing and record-keeping make these data especially unreliable for certain states, such as Indonesia.

Source: https://ourworldindata.org/covid-cases

Politics: Regime Type Is Inconclusive

The pandemic triggered novel contests and revelations. Regime type proved a poor indicator of how states fared, although the experience tended to amplify inclinations. How regimes react to "the catalytic effects of crises" (Chan 2013, 201) reflects such factors as parties and organized interests, the state's institutional structure, ideology as source of models and assumptions, and the state's geopolitical position – factors that Gourevitch (1986) emphasizes in his classic, *Politics in Hard Times*. Also germane is the extent to which the crisis reflects long-present socio-political "pathogens," such as structural inequities (Boin et al. 2016, 5).

But the evidence as to whether authoritarianism or democracy writ large is more advantageous for pandemic-management is inconclusive (e.g. Fenner 2020; Petersen 2020). The efficacy of governmental responses rests more on specific dimensions, such as the reach and effectiveness of state institutions (Fukuyama 2020; Greer et al. 2020, 3); "proactive leadership" (Fenner 2020); or federalism and decentralization, which might either hinder responsiveness by generating conflict across administrative tiers, or enhance it by allowing local authorities flexibility to adapt to on-the-ground conditions (Aubrecht et al. 2020; Greer et al. 2020, 2).

The evidence merely muddies the picture. Chinese experience, for instance, seems to demonstrate the advantages of authoritarianism in bringing the pandemic under control (see Lu 2020), at least until the debilitating strain of megacity-wide lockdowns, stretching well into 2022. On the other hand, counter-examples including Japan, Taiwan, South Korea, Australia, and New Zealand highlight the utility of "transparency, public trust and collaboration" (Berengaut 2020). Countervailing experience in Hong Kong supports that premise: the pandemic coincided with surging political protests against Chinese violations of local autonomy and freedom that eroded public trust, including in public-health mandates and advice (Matus et al. 2023).

Further complicating assessment, a comparatively illiberal regime might selectively adopt "democratic" best-practices. For example, whereas China suppressed information about the virus in its early stages, Singapore's government opted for transparency in communicating virus risks and responses (Lazar 2020). Firmly undemocratic Vietnam, too, shared rather than hoarded information, "highlight[ing] the importance of both upward and downward coordination" (Nguyen and Malesky 2021), and invited scientists and outside observers to analyze data for patterns in infections and interventions (Nguyen 2020). Yet even as surveillance capacity proved an asset in curbing contagion (Willoughby 2021, 128), public-health officials violated patients' privacy, to the extent of revealing names, addresses, and contact information. Lao officials, too, were relatively transparent in documenting cases (Meagher 2020). Meanwhile, the formally more democratic Philippines muzzled civil liberties for waves of extravagantly strict and prolonged "community quarantine" – and remained among the region's worst performers, nevertheless (See 2021).

What do these observations tell us about pandemic governance? Unfortunately little. There is indeed reason for concern about the legacies of the pandemic in narrowing space for democratic politics; I return to this issue in Section 3. However, the evidence suggests that regime type and (il)liberal trajectory reveal little about a state's capacity and efficacy in addressing the pandemic. Other factors must be at play in shaping states' approaches.

Policy: Past Pandemic Experience

The response to COVID-19 in Southeast Asia and elsewhere "covered the entire policy spectrum" (Djalante et al 2020). State actions ranged from sophisticated contact tracing, hard lockdowns, and decisive border closures to letting community transmission percolate, flexible quarantine rules, and vacillating travel restrictions.[5] The basic message of pandemic control is straightforward: policy choices that prioritize public health above economic concerns, clear and consistent public communications, and early, firm control of borders and movement all contribute to keeping a virus in check (Meagher 2020).

Policies, of course, emerge in context. A second key thread in the COVID-19 literature traces the formative influence of the 2003 SARS epidemic on present-day decisionmakers in East and Southeast Asian states. Lessons learned then clearly blazed a trail for authorities especially in Singapore, Vietnam, South Korea, Taiwan, and Hong Kong – countries with different institutional frameworks and regime types that all swung quickly into effective action. As early as December 2019, Singapore started monitoring the outbreak in Wuhan and put a "SARS strategy" in place, at a time when other countries still dismissed the outbreak as nothing more than a seasonal flu (Meagher 2020). By early February 2020, Singapore had introduced border controls and surveillance, conducted laboratory research on the new virus, halted inbound flights from China, and developed a fast, reliable system for mass testing and contact-tracing. On a similar timeline, Vietnam, too, instituted province-wide and more targeted quarantines, closed nonessential businesses, shut schools, and imposed population-surveillance measures, via a web of informants (Searight 2020). Singapore and Vietnam had been the countries in the region SARS hit

---

[5] See www.csis.org/programs/southeast-asia-program/projects/southeast-asia-covid-19-tracker#National%20Responses for policy responses by country.

hardest; now both demonstrated experience and capacity in crafting "highly centralized, unified, and well-organized" responses (Searight 2020).

The legacy of SARS extended to the regional level. Despite its norm of noninterference, the Association of Southeast Asian Nations (ASEAN) developed a shared understanding that contagions are "security threats" that require member countries to act in concert. This approach carried global resonance, with roots in earlier "disease-specific interventions" (rather than broad public-health strengthening) to address HIV, framed in terms of international health security, then also shocks from anthrax attacks to Ebola – other diseases with "potential to do damage to wealthy countries' interests" (Wenham et al. 2023, 436). The securitization of infectious diseases in the 2000s pressed ASEAN countries to accept responsibility to detect, report, and prevent cross-border spread, facilitated by ASEAN's norm-building capacity and informal networks, alongside formal mechanisms (Davies 2019). Recalling SARS, as well as other previous episodes of avian and swine influenza, relevant ASEAN platforms swung into action by early 2020. The ASEAN Pandemic Preparedness and Response project, for example, ensured that member states crafted baseline pandemic protocols, while ASEAN's Guidelines on the Provision of Emergency Assistance helped as member states repatriated each other's citizens (H.-L. Tan 2020).

That said, experience of SARS is an uneven predictor, at best, of pandemic governance. Not only does it not tell us what measures specifically states put in place, but it seems not to have honed the practices of all states equally. Within Southeast Asia, the Philippines was the next-worst SARS-affected country[6] – granted, by a substantial margin – yet it fumbled its way through this new public-health crisis, evincing none of the dexterity of experience. More problematic still, China not only suffered by far the greatest number of SARS cases and deaths globally but drew flak then, as this time, for its "lack of transparency, inaccurate information, and lack of coordination between central and local authorities," and overall "fragmented and opaque" response (Lee and McKibben 2012, 21). Clearly, "muscle memory" from past crises is insufficient to explain how states respond to an emerging epidemic.

Culture: The (Re)turn to Asian Values

In a dispatch from Thailand, *New York Times* Southeast Asia bureau chief Hannah Beech (2020) pondered, "Can the country's low rate of coronavirus infections be attributed to culture? Genetics? Face masks? Or a combination of all three?" Her response spotlighted an expert who proposed that it must be the

---

[6] See www.loc.gov/resource/g3201e.ct001290/?r=-0.152,-0.025,1.27,0.699,0.

culture of greeting each other without "body contact" that spared the people of the Mekong region from the worst of the pandemic. While this widely shared article (illustrated, perversely, with images of face-shield-wearing monks, plastic-screened school desks, face-masked park visitors, and hazard-suited workers disinfecting a market) can be viewed as typical of Western media's resort to culturally reductionist answers, it represents an enduring approach to Southeast Asia, including in studies of COVID-19: framing the region's success through the lens of Asian cultures.

This approach builds on the idea that Asian societies place greater importance on collective well-being than individual freedoms – that a communitarian rather than individualistic impulse guides socio-political behavior (Chua 1995). In the 1990s, states used this premise to justify restrictive policies on privacy, free speech, and assembly. Collective harmony, not personal liberties, is the region's ticket to economic development (and, in a pandemic, to public health), argue proponents of this cultural explanation (see Thompson 2001 for a review). Indeed, social cohesion and horizontal trust do remain higher in East and Southeast Asia, on average, than elsewhere (Tiberghien 2021, 37–38).

The evergreen focus on Asian values revived with attention to a "collective spirit" that facilitates compliance with state infection-control policies (Huang et al. 2020). Evidence included the public's acquiescing to tech-enabled surveillance such as Singapore's TraceTogether or Malaysia's MySejahtera app and supporting lockdown measures and travel bans. A 2020 YouGov survey found that Southeast Asian societies generally did demonstrate higher levels of public adherence to government protocols, such as avoiding crowded areas and wearing face masks, than did counterparts in the United States, United Kingdom, or much of Europe.[7] (Masking to avoid spreading germs has long been more common in parts of Asia than elsewhere.) Economist Jeffrey Sachs, for one, attributes successful pandemic-management in the region to a combination of top-down government policies, especially nonpharmaceutical interventions (e.g. border controls, mask mandates, quarantine rules), and the bottom-up public acquiescence to comply. This mix reflects, he suggests, "higher readiness to adopt pro-social health-seeking behaviors based on social norms and better scientific understanding of the pandemic" (Sachs 2021).

Yet some states in the region performed exceedingly poorly, were only initially lucky, or (a very real concern) did not test at sufficient levels for low positivity or mortality rates to mean much. Sachs (2021) premises his case on the "far lower mortality rate" from COVID-19 in the Asia-Pacific than in North

---

[7] See time-series data by country at https://yougov.co.uk/topics/international/articles-reports/2020/03/17/personal-measures-taken-avoid-covid-19.

America, the UK, or the EU – a difference not reducible to urbanization, climate, economic structure, population age-structure, presence of comorbidities, or other possible alternative explanations. The data he presents actually show a fair bit of spread across the Asia-Pacific, especially for those measures (e.g. quarantining inbound airline passengers) that involve government action rather than individual behavior. And that Southeast Asian cases clustered high on face-mask use from early on, for instance, could also reflect recent and ongoing experience of "haze" or air pollution, especially from burning. Meanwhile the relative dearth of "large-scale protests" against lockdowns he tallies in Asia versus Europe could manifest less a communal mindset than curbed civil liberties and differing protest repertoires.

Regardless, culture and values featured heavily in everyday political discourse in the region. In the Philippines, for instance, common rhetoric blamed a spike in COVID-19 cases on *pasaway* (recalcitrant) citizens, often associated with poor communities, bent on flouting lockdown restrictions. This cultural justification – that some Filipinos are naturally pasaway – offered cover for securitization of the pandemic. Suggests Karl Hapal (2021, 226), protecting "virtuous," law-abiding citizens from infection justified "policing and punishing" those who were not, echoing the logic of President Rodrigo Duterte's brutal war on drugs. These assumptions and resultant policy approaches, one could argue, are manifestations of "paternalistic states" that demand obedience and loyalty from their people, in exchange for the state's protection from collective threats (see Barr 2000).

Compliance with COVID-19 directives, however, cannot be reduced to a "culture of surveillance" in Vietnam – where the aforementioned YouGov data actually suggest less pandemic-related behavior change than elsewhere in the region – or to a "nanny state" in Singapore that legitimizes state intrusion in people's everyday lives (Searight 2020). "Culture" could operate through quite different, and potentially countervailing, mechanisms. Sociologist Hang Kei Ho (2020), for instance, reminds us of the prevalence in the region of "scientific states," or countries with highly educated populations who value scientific knowledge. The OECD's Programme on International Student Assessment (PISA) – a measure of scientific knowledge and skills – finds that some Southeast Asian states (notably, Singapore and Vietnam) outperform North American counterparts, even if others (Indonesia, the Philippines, Thailand) do worse. Sachs (2021) finds a correlation between a country's PISA score and compliance with COVID-19 rules. To wit, Singapore and China had the highest PISA scores and were among the countries with the highest perceived observance of COVID-19 rules, whereas Indonesia ranked lowest in the region in both PISA scores and compliance. This perspective implies why Indonesia's agriculture minister, together with other self-styled social-media influencers, could get traction in announcing fake COVID-19 cures, such as wearing eucalyptus-oil sachets to kill the virus (see Paddock 2020): lower capacity for evaluating (anti-)scientific claims leaves Indonesia comparatively more vulnerable than, say, Singapore, to an "infodemic."

Sachs was careful not to read too much into his results, but they nevertheless add nuance. Compliance with COVID-19 rules may reflect cultures of deference, to some extent, but could also reflect cultures that value scientific knowledge and rational risk assessment – or both, as culture is hardly monolithic within a given state. But the very range across these attributes within the region calls further into question the explanatory power of an Asia-Pacific-wide cultural argument. The combination of ambiguous posited effects and uncertain causality makes culture a poor predictor of pandemic governance, however colorful the explanations it suggests.

3 What Shaped Southeast Asian States' Performance

What offers greater explanatory leverage than regime type, past policy experience, or culture is deeper-set and more contingent path-dependency. Shaping policy environments are longer historical trajectories and institutional structures – and in this region especially, formative experience of developmental statehood, how authority has come to be distributed, and citizens' learned trust in, or skepticism of, leaders' intentions. Overall, I argue that the extent of concentrated rather than devolved authority in public-health planning (if less in service-delivery), how strongly the public good maintains sway over private interest, and whether authorities can count on quasi-voluntary rather than coerced compliance with directives proved key indicators for successful pandemic governance. In Southeast Asia, these features are largely legacies of developmental statehood (though, of course, different patterns of state-building may produce them, too). And while history matters, deviations from even a well-trodden path still happen, as Malaysia, which entered a new phase of political disintegration coincident with the start of the pandemic, demonstrates.

State capacity offers an entry point into these dimensions, but matters especially when approached in terms of who makes, implements, and enforces decisions, and how, rather than simply as a matter of resources. One might ask whether a basic measure of relative socioeconomic development – or, given the nature of the issues at hand, development of healthcare infrastructure specifically – really offers about as much leverage as one can hope to muster. Put briefly, measures of absolute and relative levels of healthcare spending *do* offer analytical utility, but prove blunt tools at best in explaining cross-case differences. It is not just raw capacity per se that matters but how states organize authority over it, and the interface between state and society.

Developmental States

One may note a provocative correspondence between elements of the developmental-state model in the 1960s–1990s, as well as more recent variants, and what allowed states to achieve high levels of citizen compliance and pandemic-containment, while mitigating economic and other externalities. This history is germane for the experience it conferred of central-government leadership, coordinated state action, and robust popular trust in government to deliver positive results – with the caveat that some states' paths skirted full adoption or have since veered far off-course. Especially important to these outcomes have been developmental-state hallmarks of state capacity and insulation.

The goal or reality of developmental statehood dominated the literature on East and Southeast Asian political economy through the 1980s and early 1990s (Haggard 2018 offers a succinct overview). The full-fledged model first really took root in Japan in the 1950s (see the foundational Johnson 1982), then in similarly late-developing South Korea and Taiwan by the 1960s–1970s, as it edged toward Southeast Asia: Singapore most fully, but also more aspirationally Malaysia, Thailand, and even (with generous concept-stretching) Indonesia. More recent evolution in East Asia has been toward emphasizing "capability expansion" as increasingly central to development (Evans 2014, 84–85). These states, now democracies, have shifted from earlier productivity-centered motivations for enhancing human capital, toward reconfigured state–society ties, extending beyond industrial elites (Wong 2004).

The states on which I focus range from best-fit Singapore to what is essentially a negative case – a "'non-developmental' political monopoly" (Evans and Heller 2019, 120): the Philippines. As the moniker suggests, the defining attribute is the role of the state in development policy. The model, of course, though, entails more than just that. Observers tended to conflate high growth with developmental statehood even in Asian newly industrializing countries (NICs) missing key criteria, or where rent-seeking and other predation – debilitating in Indonesia and the Philippines – clearly prevailed.

Developmental statehood was and remains heterodox; "it challenged received wisdom about the appropriate policies for achieving rapid economic growth and the institutions – and politics – for getting there" (Haggard 2018, 2). The literature as it took shape focused neither on such institutions as property rights and rule of law previously touted as keys to growth nor on formal politics, but on "the autonomy or insulation of the government from rent-seeking private interests, delegation to lead agencies, and coherent bureaucracies," then increasingly also on "the relationship between the state, the private sector, and labor organizations that appeared politically subordinated and tightly controlled" (Haggard 2018, 3). At the model's core were state bureaucracies that centered public service and meritocracy, embedded within society by "a dense set of concrete interpersonal ties," albeit more to "private entrepreneurial elites" than to civil society (Evans and Heller 2019, 111–112). This political framework put governance substantially in the hands of bureaucrats more immune to electoral or other pressures than politicians; the state was "centralized, internally coherent, and politically insulated" (Haggard 2018, 45).

In contrast to neoclassical economics, the developmental state saw "market-conforming policies" and exports as less central than governments' capacity for "coordinating private sector activity, intervening in markets, and providing selective and conditional support to firms" (Haggard 2015, 40, 42). Indeed, Haggard (2018, 7) sums up the core of the developmental state tradition, as "self-consciously opposed to dominant liberal models and favorably disposed to state intervention: in mobilizing savings and investment and in influencing the sectoral allocation of resources through planning, trade, and industrial policies, and strategic use of the financial system."

Not just how states intervened in markets mattered but also having a bureaucratic structure and political system that allowed the state to "discipline" and motivate the private sector. Industrial policy served to signal the government's credible commitment and intent (Haggard 2015, 50–52; Amsden 1991). The two leading strands in this political model were "strong executives" who delegated "to capable and appropriately incentivized bureaucracies" and a "relationship between the government, the private sector, and other social forces, including labor," such that "the developmental state was politically insulated, not only from the left and working class but the private sector as well" (Haggard 2018, 45). Particularly important was pairing constraints to keep labor weak, for the sake of flexibility and wage-restraint, with an inclusive-growth model, allowing improvements for those workers to welfare and, especially, education, as compensation (Haggard 2015, 55 and 2018, 93; also Deyo 1989).

Indeed, East Asian developmental states embraced social-security programs comparatively early on, as part of development strategy, though the contours and scope of those policies changed over time (Kwon 2007, 1). Driving adoption was neither working-class mobilization nor labor/left-wing parties, but "historically conservative," yet "ideologically flexible," catch-all incumbent parties (Wong

2025, 42–43). Ian Holliday (2000) terms this model "productivist," for its focus on growth and subordination of welfare to economic policy – inclusive of facilitative (Hong Kong), developmental-universalist (Japan, South Korea, Taiwan), and developmental-particularist (Singapore) subtypes – in contradistinction to Esping-Anderson's (1990) well-known "three worlds" of liberal, corporatist, and social-democratic welfare regimes.

Recent shifts represent a reorientation of development strategy as the service sector has overtaken manufacturing in driving growth: states must "focus more intensely on people and their skills, instead of on machines and their owners" (Evans 2014, 86). East Asian developmental states' approach has come to reflect their acknowledgment of human development as not just a product of but also an input into economic growth, and as something for which private investment will not suffice. In enhancing "capabilities," social or welfare policy becomes "essential to income growth," even though as levels of human development increase and level off, measuring and comparing capability becomes harder (Evans 2014, 87–90, 92). Key to the "21st-century developmental state," Peter Evans (2014, 90–91) explains, are "competent, coherent public bureaucracies" able to deliver relevant public services; the state's ability to sidestep elites' and elites organizations' particularistic demands in pursuit of collective goals; dense ties that "embed" the state's political and administrative apparatus within "a broad cross-section of civil society," to facilitate information-gathering and engagement; and "state effectiveness" as now "even more clearly a political problem." These efforts ensure a competent and hale labor force, but extend increasingly beyond that baseline, where industrial strategy and its underlying ethos have changed.

In practice, though, social-protection policies have always been selective. Favoring the industrial workers at the core of development plans – those who paid into social benefits, eschewing over-dependence on the state – "developmental welfare state" policies initially bypassed informal-sector workers or income-support benefits such as unemployment insurance, reinforcing economic inequality (Kwon 2007, 2-3). States have adjusted their welfare-policy mixes over time, as they confront a postindustrial (and post-state-led-development) political economy and in response to shocks such as the Asian financial crisis of 1997–1998 but also with electoral sparring and bottom-up pressure following political liberalization (Wong 2025). Nevertheless, retooling remains incomplete, at best. Developmental welfare states remain gender-biased and still exclude much of the temporary or irregular workforce. They remain, too, less redistributive than the Nordic ideal, financed still mostly through workers' social-insurance premiums (Kwon 2007, 13; Wong 2025, 2).

Table 2 Developmental state attributes, at their peak

	Centralization of economic policymaking	Ability to marshal financial and labor resources	Autonomous, politically insulated bureaucracy	Insulation from rent-seeking
Singapore	Strong	Strong	Strong	Strong
Malaysia	Strong	Strong	Moderate	Moderate
Thailand	Strong	Moderate	Moderate	Moderate
Indonesia	Moderate	Weak	Moderate	Weak
Philippines	Moderate	Weak	Weak	Weak

Nor have all developmental states embraced "inclusive welfare developmentalism." Notably, Singapore, still pursuing development largely through trade and finance, has confronted less political or economic restructuring since the 1980s than Korea or Taiwan, and thus less pressure to expand social policies beyond paid-in pensions and housing. It maintains instead "selective welfare developmentalism" (Kwon 2007, 4–12). Any assessment of the legacies of developmental statehood needs thus to take into account not just policies at the model's peak but also shifts in context, relative adaptation over time, and the processes that generate such adaptation.

More broadly, not all states glossed as "developmental" adopted the framework's signature policies fully or exclusively, or did so thanks to the same institutional impetuses or social coalitions (Haggard 2015, 40). Table 2 suggests, at a broad-brush level, how closely the polities on which I focus here have, at least historically, approximated developmental states. All made at least some effort – the Philippines generally later than the others – to initiate state-led industrialization and development planning. However, they possessed in differing degrees the hallmark attributes of the development state, including sufficient fiscal and human resource capacity to implement state-led plans, but especially the ability to eschew electorally motivated decision-making, rent-seeking (whether from politicians or well-connected private actors), patronage politics, and cronyistic or nepotistic favoritism. (For more on the extent to which each state approximates the developmental-state ideal, see Routley 2012, 10–11 or Doner, Ritchie, and Slater 2005.)

Moreover, not only has political liberalization made the least progress in the most developmental of Southeast Asian states, but these states overall have diverged from East Asian counterparts in their social-protection efforts. The norm, Rosser and Murphy (2023) argue, has been layering on limited innovations, primarily to education and healthcare, and favoring public- and formal-sector employees, rather than embracing inclusive welfare developmentalism. That tendency reflects, in part, permeation of technocratic, economic-growth-focused productivism, but also, in part, stronger predatory political interests than progressive ones.

Political transformation may be especially important in a domain such as healthcare, even if relevant technocrats or specialists retain privileged voice. Democracy itself, through various mechanisms (elections, exercise of civil liberties, etc.), usually benefits public health: states provide, and citizens use, health-enhancing services (McGuire 2020). Yet *how* that correlation develops varies, warranting close attention to policy processes. In Thailand, for instance, as in other democratizing states, explains Joseph Harris (2017), doctors and lawyers mobilized in "professional movements" (e.g. Thailand's Rural Doctors' Society in the 1990s–2000s), capitalizing on political competition to press universal healthcare onto party platforms and policy agendas. Their specific expertise and commitment could counter conservative domestic and international pushback, including from a stridently opposed medical establishment. These efforts complemented more grassroots social-movement advocacy to expand access to specific lifesaving treatments. Beyond the electoral fray proper, similarly reformist, public-minded bureaucrats (including medical professionals within ministries) may institutionalize such inputs, or themselves innovate strategically for cognate goals. Harris (2015) terms this process "developmental capture" of the state. Outside linkages, with both domestic civil society and international backers, reinforce these bureaucrats' political insulation and autonomy (169).

Clearly, not all features of contemporary states that align with developmentalist praxis trace their lineage to a developmental-state history. Relative (de)centralization, for instance, may reflect subsequent decisions and strategies. Yet even in those instances, it is plausible that lessons of what "worked" in terms of past developmental-state efforts, there or elsewhere, still informed policy choices. Furthermore, some segments of any bureaucracy better approximate than others a Weberian bureaucratic ethos of commitment to the public good over other social relationships. One should expect, instead, particularly in states inclined toward clientelism, a "patchwork" assemblage, developed over time, of organizational capacities and performance (McDonnell 2020, 6–9). What is key to this literature – and to this return to the model now – is less "discrete causal variables" than "how features of these polities and societies combined or were configured in ways that promoted economic growth" as well as the impetus to take "history seriously" (Haggard 2015, 41).

In the COVID-19 era, states' focus was not economic growth per se, however trenchant the challenge of postpandemic economic recovery. But indications are that the institutions that enabled strong and protracted growth, or their legacies, allowed state coordination and societal cooperation, increasing the odds of success in confronting this very different challenge. The question is not whether the developmental state geared back into action, notwithstanding countervailing effects of economic and political liberalization (Haggard 2018, 89–90), but how that experience and its institutional residue prepare a government and society to act. Certain of these features may overlap with simple illiberal leadership. Indeed, the "East Asian miracle" sparked alternative explanations centered on regime type – that authoritarian states were better able to marshal resources, overcome rent-seeking, and coax business and labor into compliance, without worrying about popular push-back. Still, Japan's (democratic) example aside, cross-national data, including of developmentally inept autocracies, debunked that hypothesis (Haggard 2018, 47–50). As will become apparent, too, coercive control is suboptimal to at least quasi-voluntary compliance when it comes to matters of public health.

Mark Beeson's (2010, 278) framing of the effects of "developmental experience" for Southeast Asia is compelling: not just a propensity for authoritarianism but also in terms of broader issues of governance (for him, addressing environmental challenges). Most important in this vein are, simply, different popular expectations of the government's role: the strong record of growth Asia's developmental model provided "revolved around a powerful, interventionist state" (279). Democratization, he finds, may diminish administrative capacity (279), whatever its other benefits; also, states obliged to take political consequences seriously may be hard-pressed to adopt necessary harsh steps, or may suspend ordinary rules to do so under cover of extraordinary measures. Permeation of an ideological framework supportive of the state's taking the lead to spearhead industry efforts, to coordinate across sectors, and to compel (generally without needing to coerce) compliance marks this framework and legacy as salient.

Two features of a developmental-state legacy, related both to economic structures and political organization, are particularly salient to pandemic governance. First and foremost is *state capacity*, reflecting both centralized coordination and resources – that is, the first two columns in Table 2. Most obviously germane is the state's role in public health, with a high level of centralization in policymaking, even if with a degree of distributed agency in healthcare provision. Indeed, notwithstanding compelling arguments for decentralization of service delivery, centralized planning proved valuable for a multifaceted response to the virus and resulting externalities. The state's role in infrastructure is also relevant: quick rollout of systems ranging from contract-tracing technology to border controls to pharmaceuticals and test-kits benefits from a centralized authority able to organize resources and set a course quickly. The second feature, reflecting more political character than economic facility (the latter two columns in Table 2), is *insulation* from popular pressure and political or particularistic interests. An emphasis on, and bureaucratic structure conducive to, curbing rent-seeking and corruption proved particularly valuable, given the scope of pandemic relief packages and services rolled out in short order. And all presumes a shared ideological perspective regarding the optimal relationship between state and society.

State capacity resists easy metrics. Available resources offer a first cut. Assessed in terms of relative wealth and development, the countries considered here span a wide range. Yet even allowing for variations in testing capabilities and commitment, these measures correlated poorly, even counterintuitively, with infection totals or rates at different points in the pandemic. World Bank data from pandemic-eve 2019 offer gross national income per capita figures (PPP, in current international dollars) ranging from $9,860 for the Philippines, to $10,630 for Vietnam, $11,750 for Indonesia, $19,290 for Thailand, $28,730 for Malaysia, and $93,310 for Singapore.[8] (That sequence and scale of variation generally holds across indicators.) Yet it is not just the wealthiest countries that performed best in terms of case-counts: Vietnam indubitably outperformed wealthier neighbors.

More robust human development index[9] (HDI) values tell a similar story. Singapore ranked 9th globally, with a "very high" HDI value in 2019 of 0.94. Malaysia fell lower in that bracket, at 57th globally; its HDI value was 0.81. Thailand was in the "high" bracket, tied at 79th, with a value of 0.78. The Philippines and Indonesia were also in "high": tied for 107th place, both with a value of 0.72. Vietnam was near the bottom of that bracket, tied for 117th at 0.70.[10] Again, strong HDI (e.g. Malaysia) is no assurance of either effective pandemic-management or contained economic fallout, though robust national reserves (particularly germane for Singapore) *do* afford a government greater leverage in its response.

But especially germane here are measures of public-health capacity specifically, including for dealing with crises. Assessments of healthcare provision overlap this measure, but commonly include also private-sector involvement. In late 2019, Johns Hopkins University, working with the Economist Intelligence Unit, developed a Global Health Security Index, in part designed to measure states' capacity to manage exactly the sort of pandemic they confronted just a few months later. Their measures track only partially with

---

[8] https://data.worldbank.org.
[9] HDI includes indicators for life expectancy at birth, education, and standard of living.
[10] https://hdr.undp.org/en/composite/HDI.

the unfolding of the pandemic across Southeast Asia. Among 195 countries in the index, Southeast Asian cases ranked relatively well: Thailand came in 6th overall, Malaysia 18th, Singapore 24th, Indonesia 30th, Vietnam 50th, and the Philippines 53rd (Johns Hopkins 2019, 20, 22). Those placements align poorly with subsequent pandemic severity across these cases and understate the spread among them. Thailand was the highest-ranked middle-income country in the index and a standout globally, a score the report attributed to its strong health system, broad access to that system, and excellent tracking and tracing capacities (Johns Hopkins 2019, 55). Since the 1990s, Thailand has been working aggressively to scale up its disease-control capabilities, under a national-security (albeit also regional-security) frame (Wenham 2018); this placement was, hence, perhaps unsurprising. Vietnam, among the most successful countries globally in managing this pandemic (notwithstanding a mid-2021 surge), ranked relatively modestly. The lowest scoring Southeast Asian countries on the health-security index were Cambodia at 89 and Timor-Leste at 166; both performed swimmingly until around March 2021.

Nor do COVID-19 testing levels, let alone vaccination levels, as more focused indicators for public-health capacity, adequately explain evident variation. No Southeast Asian states except Singapore were testing or vaccination exemplars, in global terms. And problems of vaccine access that had plagued efforts to address past disease outbreaks (Fidler 2010) remained entrenched. Cost alone kept high-quality mRNA vaccines out of less-wealthy countries' reach, here as elsewhere.[11] But one does see substantial range, both across cases and within states over time. As Table 1 indicates, rates for testing correlated at least loosely with resources available – highest here is Singapore, followed by Malaysia; Vietnam and Indonesia lagged dramatically – but not with the overall case-fatality rate (i.e. one's odds of surviving the virus). Moreover, reliable data are not available for much of Southeast Asia (Brunei, Cambodia, Laos, Myanmar, Timor-Leste), and may be dubious for other states – for example, for Indonesia, given especially low testing levels coincident with distressingly high (albeit also unreliable) excess-deaths numbers (Lindsey and Walden 2021).[12] In other words, national wealth is helpful in affording testing, vaccines, and the best possible medical care for those who do contract the virus; investing heavily in health infrastructure (Table 3) *should* thus correlate with better

---

[11] China's Sinovac was a more-available alternative – but in Thailand, at least, that a Thai conglomerate was a business partner diminished public confidence (Rosser and Murphy 2023, 24).
[12] Our World in Data (https://ourworldindata.org/covid-cases) offers several measures of excess mortality; *Economist* 2021 offers additional, well-explained data (mixing cities and countries), highlighting where data are missing. On the vagaries of pandemic-related data broadly: Greer et al. 2021, 6-7.

Table 3 Healthcare spending and capacity, as of 2011–2019

	Vietnam	Philippines	Indonesia	Thailand	Malaysia	Singapore
GDP per capita (current USD)	2,715.30	3,485.10	4,135.60	7,806.70	11,414.20	65,233.30
Healthcare expenditure, % GDP	5.92	4.4	2.87	3.79	3.76	4.46
Health expenditure per capita (current USD)	151.69	136.54	111.68	275.92	427.22	2,823.64
Hospital beds per 1,000 pop.	2.6	1.0	1.0	2.1	1.9	2.5
Physicians per 1,000 pop.	0.8	0.6	0.4	0.8	1.5	2.3

Source: https://data.worldbank.org

outcomes, in terms of infections and deaths. Part of the useful legacy of successful developmental-statehood is arguably simply creating state wealth that a well-insulated bureaucracy can deploy effectively. But these patterns are noticeable less consistently than they are at the margins, nor can they explain fluctuations in the course of the pandemic within states over time.

What matters is less the amount spent than how it is coordinated – here is where developmental-state legacies, melding capacity with insulation, really enter the frame. It bears reiterating, though, the extent to which Southeast Asia's social-protection systems, across state configurations, "continue to have strong conservative, productivist and predatory attributes" (Rosser and Murphy 2023, 2). A closer look at a few cases will help to clarify.

Singapore is an obvious outlier in the region. Its healthcare infrastructure is exemplary overall, as befitting its high-income status (but see Barr 2008 for a critical take). That strength also reflects both longstanding efforts of the dominant People's Action Party (PAP) to justify its rule by providing high-quality public goods – ensuring welfare secures electoral support, as well as the workforce needs of a state developmental strategy (Kwon 2007). The PAP has governed since independence, bolstered by curbs on civil liberties and opposition parties, but also by compelling ideological messaging and widespread satisfaction with what the PAP government has achieved for Singapore and Singaporeans (see Tan 2018, 4–20).

Across Singapore, healthcare is normally accessible at the neighborhood level and affordable. Health policy and administration are centralized, though specific towns might opt to develop particular niches (e.g. expanded senior-care facilities where residents trend older).[13] Especially important as the pandemic developed was the Singapore government's emphasis on increasing transparency in order to ensure compliance with public-health orders, with the fundamentally technocratic assumption that if the public understood both what the guidelines required and the urgency of following them, they would do their part. The extent to which Singapore's government counted on public trust in their leadership comes through in the contrast with Indonesia, where, early in the pandemic, President Joko Widodo admitted that his government was withholding information about cases: "we did not deliver certain information to the public because we did not want to stir panic" (Pangestika 2020).

That said, quality-of-life and safety mandates that apply to the population in general in Singapore exclude work-permit holders – fixed-term migrant workers – to keep labor costs low. The Singapore state largely leaves it to private employers

---

[13] Fortuitously, the government had opened a 330-bed, state-of-the-art National Centre for Infectious Diseases in 2019.

to ensure the welfare of migrant workers in their employ. Not only did prevention efforts, including even distribution of hand-sanitizer and masks, thus not extend to these workers, but the charity that runs the volunteer-staffed, low-cost clinics on which migrant workers usually rely reduced services by 90 percent and closed two of three locations once the government announced measures in early February 2020 to consolidate healthcare workers in one hospital for COVID-19 care (Geddie and Aravindam 2020). This lacuna proved a serious liability, as more than 90 percent of Singapore's cases came to be among migrant workers, mostly in overcrowded worker dormitories (McDonald 2021). The government ultimately bore the brunt of testing and treatment costs; migrant workers still benefited from Singapore's excellent healthcare.

The case shows starkly how essentially distinctions premised on a developmentalist orientation, in which migrant labor represents a (human) capital input, complicate the translation of capacity into public-health outcomes. In seeking to minimize particularism or partisanship in favor of a purported shared national interest, defined largely in terms of economic growth, the model lends predictability and constancy. But it may be less well-suited for capturing segments that require a bespoke (and stigma-free) approach – in the context of a pandemic, returned or trapped-abroad migrant workers, or informal-economy workers. Hence, the holes in the net the Singapore government cast in managing outbreaks there.

Nonetheless, Singapore's developmentalist orientation – not just available resources but also the government's ability to command their deployment – positioned the government well to act on lessons it learned from the SARS outbreak (and tested and reinforced in light of H1N1 in 2009 and Zika in 2016).[14] In 2003, Singapore launched a cross-agency task force, reactivated in 2020, to coordinate intervention and messaging. Contact-tracing, for instance, mobilized the Ministry of Health and the police for joint efforts; the government also linked up with the country's state-supported biomedical research community. Speedily developed diagnostic tools and tests, including effective, quick-turnaround swab tests, facilitated Singapore's contagion-control efforts. The state designated and equipped around 1,000 private clinics as Public Health Preparedness Clinics – an innovation from efforts to address recurrent severe air-pollution episodes and H1N1. Singapore citizens and permanent residents paid only a token fee for diagnosis and treatment. Should they test positive, the government covered hospitalization and other costs. Close contacts of those testing positive were quarantined; individuals returning from countries experiencing community spread faced a mandatory, enforced stay-home notice

---

[14] This overview draws primarily on Li and Tan 2020.

(SHN). A daily allowance for self-employed Singaporeans cushioned the impact of quarantine. These rules evolved with phases of the pandemic and vaccine roll-outs. Such measures required high state capacity, including both financial resources and surveillance and enforcement capacity. They also relied upon established links with research and industry, minimal rent-seeking, plus public compliance, building on a high degree of public trust.

Indonesia offers an illuminating contrast, highlighting how much not just state capacity but also *insulation* of decision-making matters. Though Indonesia consistently ranks relatively low in terms of proportion of GDP spent on health, as well as in measures such as hospital beds per capita (see Table 3), its healthcare system has undergone considerable reform over the last two decades. Notably, Indonesia has massively expanded public coverage, culminating with the establishment of a universal healthcare insurance scheme in 2014, which *The Economist* magazine described as "building the biggest 'single-payer' national health scheme ... in the world" (*Economist* 2012). Indonesia has also expanded capacity, as measured by numbers of primary-healthcare centers, hospitals, and healthcare workers. It fared exceptionally well in the aforementioned Global Health Security Index in the category of "commitments to improving national capacity, financing and adherence to norms," ranking 7th globally (Johns Hopkins 2019, 21).

However noteworthy these improvements, problems in quality and consistency of healthcare remain significant. For example, the universal healthcare system has faced chronic problems of low collection of premiums and poor data-management, endangering its financial sustainability and producing significant coverage gaps (see, for example, Deloitte Indonesia 2019; Pramita et al. 2020). The introduction of decentralizing reforms provided impetus for local politicians to expand healthcare coverage and invest in facilities (Aspinall 2014), but it also seriously undermined coordination in the sector, worsening outcomes in some regions (Kristiansen and Santoso 2006). Most importantly, rent-seeking and corruption continue to blight the healthcare system (Rosser 2012), resulting often in either substandard services or patients' being charged illegal fees. Given such problems in the public system, private health insurance and providers remain the choice of many middle-class citizens, while the wealthy often seek treatment overseas, especially in Malaysia and Singapore. (Some of Singapore's earliest COVID-19 infections were from Indonesians seeking treatment there.)

Against this backdrop, after Indonesia recorded its first COVID-19 cases in early March 2020, the health system struggled to respond. Indonesia transitioned to democratic rule following the collapse of the authoritarian Suharto regime in 1998. Institutionally, Indonesia's executive-dominated multi-party democracy features broadly inclusive coalitions marked by a patronage-sharing logic (Slater 2018); reforms since the late 1990s have devolved significant authority to subnational regions. President Joko Widodo (known as Jokowi) secured his second term in office in April 2019. Competitive elections notwithstanding, emerging scholarly consensus deems democratic decline, percolating since shortly post-transition, to have accelerated under Jokowi (Power and Warburton 2020).[15] While observers initially viewed Jokowi as a reformer, largely for his prior record in local government, this drift toward illiberalism reflected, in part, Jokowi's single-minded focus on economic growth (Warburton 2016) – a hallmark of developmentalism, but absent an institutional structure for technocratic, insulated direction.

Reluctance to grapple with the threat the virus posed came to characterize Indonesia's response, especially during the early months. The government eventually did take steps toward containment, but they remained partial and hesitant. From the beginning, Jokowi was preoccupied with the potential economic effects for Indonesia of the slowdown in world trade. As it became evident that the virus was spreading domestically, his concern shifted to the potential economic effects (eventually confirmed to be dire) of lockdown policies. Meanwhile, the country struggled to develop testing and treatment capacity. Senior officials repeatedly expressed doubt about the seriousness of the challenge. In February 2020, as foreign experts noted the likelihood of significant spread in Indonesia (Agence France-Presse 2020), Health Minister Terawan Agus Putranto attributed Indonesia's apparent invulnerability to COVID to God's blessings: "It's because of our prayers" (Cochrane 2020). As late as early April, the powerful Coordinating Minister for Investment and Maritime Affairs, Luhut Binsar Pandjaitan, stated that government modeling showed that the coronavirus would be unable to survive Indonesia's tropical climate (Hakim 2020). Overseas commentators rated the government response as sluggish and ineffective (for example, Bland 2020; Jaffrey 2020; Mietzner 2020); more tellingly, numerous Indonesian epidemiologists, public-health specialists, economists, and other experts made similar evaluations. Early on, for example, while the government – susceptible to political pressure – hesitated on shutdowns, 90 percent of Indonesian economists the Indonesian Regional Science Association surveyed stated that failure to impose quarantines and restrictions on movement would create greater economic harm than doing so (Siregar et al. 2020).

Problems with testing and contact-tracing reflected both political will and systemic weaknesses in Indonesia's health system, of both resources and

---

[15] Election of authoritarian-era general Prabowo Subianto to succeed Jokowi in 2024 offers further confirmation.

coordination. Indonesia lacked the laboratories and expertise, and failed to commit sufficient funding, to conduct testing on a mass scale. The government neglected to set a standard price for tests conducted privately – which many required to travel or work (Shalilah 2020). As a result, testing remained often prohibitively expensive. Bureaucratic roadblocks played their part, too: at a public dressing-down of cabinet ministers in June 2020, Jokowi singled out the health ministry for being particularly slow in expending funds. Nor were state efforts insulated from corruption. Most notably, Social Affairs Minister Juliari Batubara was ultimately convicted and given a twelve-year sentence for food-aid-related graft and embezzlement totaling over USD3 million (Rosser and Murphy 2023, 24). Moreover, Indonesia's vaccine rollout occurred, in part, through political parties, which received allocations essentially as patronage resources to distribute among their constituents and supporters (Sari et al. 2023). Though these impediments factored significantly in speeding the progress of the pandemic, the response also saw a great deal of regional variation – and creativity – across Indonesia. Local health authorities used the grassroots system of local health centers to reach out to and monitor potentially infected persons. (I return to that subnational innovation below.)

In short, Indonesia lacked the centralized authority, streamlined and insulated bureaucracy, inculcated public reliance on and trust in state services, and constraints on rent-seeking needed to organize a speedy and effective response. Furthermore, what strong-state legacies Indonesia might have had, democratization has undercut, such that political considerations temper policy choices. (Backsliding leaves that "democratic" classification increasingly in question, but the direction of the slide has been more toward personalism and rent-seeking than toward technocratic decision-making.)

The Philippine healthcare system offers still another model, yet again confirms the utility in a pandemic of both state capacity and bureaucratic insulation. Healthcare in the Philippines "gravitates towards two opposing doctrines of welfarism and free enterprise" (Sy 2003, 555). Public-health expenditures have increased consistently since 2005, yet per capita, remain lower than levels in Vietnam, if at least above Indonesia's (Table 3). The public and private sectors share authority: the former is funded by taxes and run by national and local governments, while the latter is a market-driven system consisting of for-profit and nonprofit healthcare providers (Dayrit, et al. 2018).

Among the services devolved to municipalities are primary healthcare, dental health, and maternal and child health. The Department of Health provides policy direction and strategic plans, as well as regulatory services and standards.

It also runs tertiary-level (specialist) public hospitals. Local governments handle primary- and secondary-level healthcare. Under the Local Government Code of 1991, they have full autonomy to manage their own programs. The Philippines' universal healthcare program, PhilHealth, covers treatment in private and government health facilities for 92 percent of the population, including 40 percent from poor populations whose premiums the government subsidizes. Yet access to healthcare is inequitable across the archipelago, "due to the maldistribution of facilities, health staff, and specialists" (Dayrit, et al. 2018, xxvi) – and provision of doctors, for example, remains well below the WHO's prescribed average of 10 per 10,000 (Table 3).

Given this system, one might expect uneven outcomes, in socioeconomic-class as well as geographic terms. The Philippines' poor performance vis-à-vis our other cases, in terms of confirmed cases, death rate, and vaccination progress seems fairly well-predicted by its healthcare investment and structure – perhaps better than overall state capacity and wealth statistics alone might indicate. The state lacks a structure conducive to ramping up an effective national response in short order.

The centerpiece of the Duterte administration's COVID-19 strategy was the Bayanihan to Heal as One Act, which granted the president emergency powers, couched in rhetoric of *bayanihan*, or mutual cooperation. However, there was "no evident systematic integration of these disparate elements into a comprehensive strategic design" (Romero 2020), and the health sector remained overburdened and underfunded. The absence of a coherent action plan became manifest in challenges medical front-liners faced. As of late April 2020, as the pandemic gained steam, medical workers comprised 13 percent of the country's COVID-19 cases, well beyond the regional average of 2–3 percent (Yee and Aurelio 2020). The Philippine Medical Association faulted frontline workers' lack of personal protective equipment. Only after eleven private hospitals put pressure on the government did it dedicate three public hospitals to serve as special COVID-19 treatment centers.

But scarce lab supplies, understaffed hospitals, and poor infrastructure continued severely to compromise the Department of Health's response. Targeted testing posed a particular challenge from the outset. Although testing rates improved by mid-2020, a year later, they still remained less than a third per capita of Malaysia's (Table 1). Using the WHO's more focused metric of testing per the scale of the epidemic in a given country (that is, overall tests relative to positive outcomes), with a target of no more than 5 percent positive tests, the Philippines still underperformed, by a lot: its daily positivity rate as of mid-June 2021 remained 14.95 percent (globally just above Indonesia, at 15.36 percent, whereas Singapore ranked the best in the world, at 0.01 percent).[16]

A May 2020 poll found that 43 percent of Filipinos expected their quality of life to worsen in the next twelve months – "the worst trend in polling history" (SWS 2020). This sentiment was not unfounded. The Philippine economy, which had sustained 6 percent GDP growth over the preceding five years, shrank for the first time in two decades in 2020, by 9.6 percent, over double the global rate of 4.3 percent (World Bank 2021b, 22, 4) and dramatically lagging other states in the region (World Bank 2021a, xii). Despite projections for positive growth, GDP continued to contract in the first quarter of 2021, by another 4.2 percent – the worst performance in the region by far – as a surge in cases "derailed the recovery momentum" (World Bank 2021b, 2). A much higher rate of "vaccine hesitancy" in the Philippines than elsewhere in the region – six in ten survey respondents in February 2021 did *not* want a vaccine, versus only 16 percent who did – as well as a delayed and fragmented plan for vaccine delivery (World Bank 2021b, 21), further complicated recovery prospects. Frustrated with resistance to vaccination (attributed largely to fallout from the botched 2016 rollout of a new dengue vaccine; Dayrit et al. 2020), and ignoring the issue of low supplies, Duterte expostulated in June 2021, "If you don't want to be vaccinated, I'll have you arrested and have the vaccine shot into your [buttocks]," or holdouts should leave the country (Cabato 2021). These polling data, and the president's outburst, suggest inconsistency in public-health messaging and problematic distrust in relevant authorities. Indeed, corruption ran rampant in a bureaucracy permeated by, rather than insulated from, rent-seeking. By May 2020, complaints of diverted relief funds and graft were sufficiently widespread that the Duterte administration offered whistleblowers cash rewards (OCCRP 2020).

In sum, state capacity broadly and healthcare capacity specifically matter a great deal, including how these endowments are structured and coordinated; their deployment reveals benefits from bureaucratic insulation, as well. Across the region, the course of the pandemic reflected in significant part how prepared each state was to engage in widespread prevention, screening, contact-tracing, and vaccination efforts; how well-equipped each was to manage positive cases in order to optimize odds of recovery and minimize further spread; and what capacity each had to implement unpopular containment measures. Doing all that well required significant financial and political resources – all the more so as

---

[16] Among Southeast Asian states for which data are available, only Cambodia at 7.57 percent and Malaysia at 6.7 percent also exceeded the WHO target. Johns Hopkins Coronavirus Resource Center, "How Does Testing in the U.S. Compare to Other Countries?" https://coronavirus.jhu.edu/testing/international-comparison (updated/accessed 18 June 2021).

shutdowns and plunging economic prospects left many individuals unable to social-distance and loath either to lose opportunities to work or to spend on protective equipment, let alone on often-costly COVID-19 tests. But one also sees the limits to what state capacity or character alone explains, given the political decisions behind prioritizing healthcare versus other spending and distribution, and the greater utility of evidence-backed approaches in building confidence, than of pandering or threats.

Taken together, these cases suggest a complex of features germane to pandemic governance. Authoritarian leanings alone are not sufficient – viz., the Philippines, where a poorly coordinated, battle-like approach bedraggled both public health and the economy. (We will return to that approach later.) Yet nor is responding to a (presumed) popular preference, lacking insulation from such pressures: Indonesia's effort not to distress the electorate with onerous controls underplayed the reality of the pandemic at a time when the state needed to take firm action, however politically risky. In both these cases, too, resource and coordination constraints compounded the challenge. Testing, treatment, and vaccines are costly, and maintaining welfare and keeping the economy afloat through prolonged lockdowns, even more so. Singapore, in contrast, had the benefit of national wealth, but also, given its developmental-state history, the bureaucratic insulation and capacity, and state authority, to marshal research, medical, business, and other resources, as well as trust-based popular compliance, for a well-choreographed, relatively agile campaign of containment and recovery – at least outside precarious communities of "human resources."

To press further, and especially to parse resources, regimes, and bureaucratic framework, I turn now to disentangling agency from structure, then to the character of state–society relations.

Distribution of Authority

As the foregoing discussion makes clear, crisis-management, including in the case of a pandemic, benefits from well-informed, efficient, politically insulated and programmatic decision-making, as well as the ability to muster resources and both political and popular will. Our cases suggest that an effective pandemic response involves top-down direction – a hallmark of developmental-state management – but with significant cooperation and coordination between national and subnational governments. Much of this region has moved toward decentralization, whether "big-bang" or incremental, since the 1980s–1990s. Decentralization is helpful insofar as it allows local innovation and responsiveness – contexts change rapidly during an emergency and may vary dramatically subnationally, so local actors need to adapt quickly. But decentralization is no panacea.

Local bright spots are insufficient when it comes to either communicable disease or encompassing economic processes, and the technical and financial imperatives of such a crisis require higher-tier direction. Governance is multi-leveled: different measures or qualities may be useful at different sites or in different sectors. Yet not only might structure and agency align poorly, but also, weaknesses in coordination, consistency, or resource-allocation may render local governments "confused," "passive," and inclined toward "localism," and the system as a whole less efficient or accountable (Vu-Thanh 2016, 189). Weaker centralization or institutionalization, on the other hand, may facilitate local adaptation when a nimble, targeted response is helpful. All told, a "spectrum" is evident, ranging from "broadly positive interactions and effective collaboration between national and local authorities"; to "cases in which relations are more compensatory, such that local strengths offset weakness at the centre or vice-versa"; to less felicitous "situations in which neither centre nor city proves able to mount an effective response to the pandemic, and/or where the two are in conflict about how best to proceed" (Weiss et al. 2021, 2-3). Yet the functional distribution of authority in a crisis may be hazy.

First and foremost, decentralization may be encoded more in structures than agency; institutional form alone does not reveal where real authority lies. In Indonesia and the Philippines – the two countries in the region where local authority is most expansive and entrenched, following far-reaching decentralizing reforms launched in the 1990s (Diokno-Sicat and Maddawin 2018; Negara and Hutchinson 2021) – it is striking that national governments (albeit to differing degrees) defaulted toward centralizing impulses. Their restricting the ability of local governments to design their own responses reflected broader illiberal and recentralizing trends in both countries (e.g. Ostwald et al. 2016, 143; Eaton, 2001, 114–22). In neither case were local authorities able to buffer substantially against central-government pathologies. Local initiative remained significant (especially in Indonesia), but notably, it was in Malaysia, where the national government was experiencing a moment of particular weakness as the pandemic percolated, that subnational authorities pushed back with greatest – and least precedented – force. In Thailand, too, institutional centralization did not preclude local innovation, though more in coordination with than in opposition to the central government (e.g. Hatchakorn and Viengrat 2021).

A second perspective on agency asks the source of relevant decisions. How much *should* one expect institutional differences to matter? It might be that variation in government responses (especially early on) is better explained by the choices of political leaders, absent strong institutional filters. In that case, one might anticipate greater inconsistency over time and with past decisions than otherwise, assuming institutions lend policy choices regularity and predictability. Through what channels policy decisions flow affects whose interests they aim to protect, and what mechanisms for interest-articulation and representation matter most. Empowered leaders, too, might be central-government or subnational politicians (or both), working in alignment or at cross-purposes, with comparable or imbalanced authority, and with or without electoral, economic, or other incentives to temper their judgment.

To probe these dimensions of central versus local, and institutions versus personal agency – to examine how decision-making authority is distributed and the relative pros and cons of different configurations – I return to my cases. To what extent have divisions of authority between national and subnational governments generally, and control over healthcare systems and budgets specifically, shaped and either enhanced or impeded outcomes? Also, who among decision-makers enforces, or might readily evade, accountability? As in considering (overlapping) developmentalist legacies, these questions of structures and agency offer further insight into how insulated public-health or economic-recovery decisionmakers are from partisan or particularistic pressures, whether state institutions (or individual leaders) command legitimacy to secure voluntary compliance with public-health measures, and the extent to which decisions across or within tiers of government align.

Structurally decentralized Indonesia and the Philippines offer particular insight. In both, enterprising local-government leaders have, at times, taken the initiative to outperform the national government. However, tension between levels has percolated since the outset of decentralization. Key relevant authority remains with the central state, not least given increasingly personalized rule, especially in the Philippines. There, members of Congress were and remain especially loath to cede credit for center-to-local fiscal transfers, given pervasively dynastic, patronage-fueled politics (Eaton 2001, 115–118). Yet in Indonesia, too, despite public support, significant decentralization barely survived its first decade, yielding mixed results at best and exacerbating "turf wars" and "money politics" (Tomsa 2015). The extent of devolution of resources and authority remains fraught, and the future of direct local-executive elections (*pilkada*) remains uncertain, amid broader dynamics of restricting competition and consolidating power in Jakarta (Baker 2023; *Tempo* 2024).

In Indonesia, patterns of subnational variation in political and economic outcomes have preoccupied social scientists over the last two decades. Decentralization of authority and resources was among the signature reforms of postauthoritarian Indonesia, producing significant disparities in political patterns and development outcomes across the archipelago. The process has generated both experimentations with good-governance measures and local-authority capture by predatory local networks (e.g. Hadiz 2010; Hill 2015).

At the same time, decentralization has occurred in a context of strong centralizing traditions, and of the national government's reserving key areas of jurisdiction and control – including the power to declare a national health emergency, which Jokowi's government did in late March 2020.

Indonesia's decentralization framework was woven into the fabric of its pandemic response, resulting in poorly coordinated policies and opaque accountability. In particular, the national government made local governments responsible for requesting partial lockdowns. Under Minister of Health Regulation No. 9/2020, regions could request permission from the ministry to implement one (termed Large-Scale Social Restrictions, PSBB), provided they could show their region met certain epidemiological conditions. (In fact, the government did not provide clear guidelines on what it meant by a "significant spread and number of cases," the key criterion.) At the same time, the national government required local governments to reallocate parts of their own budgets to the COVID-19 response, whether for health measures, social-safety-net expansion, or other efforts; the central government threatened to cut their budgetary allocations otherwise (Farisa 2020). The fact that by mid-June 2020, fifty-five regions (of 514) had still not reported their spending plans to the Interior Ministry revealed the uneven nature of the response (Mudassir 2020).

Moreover, the process generated significant conflict across levels of government, as lower tiers blamed those higher up for slow and inadequate action – highlighting the gap between structural decentralization and distribution of relevant authority (e.g. Meckelburg 2020). The most famous of these conflicts was between Jakarta governor (and Jokowi rival) Anies Baswedan, whose efforts to respond proactively by shutting down public transport and implementing other public-health measures the national government repeatedly contradicted or even cancelled (Mietzner 2020). Anies expressed frustration with the central government's slowness, including when he sought permission for a partial lockdown. He expostulated: "[It's] as if we are proposing a project that needed a feasibility study. Can't the ministry [of health] see that we are facing a rising death toll? Is it not enough?" (Syakriah 2020).

By mid-April 2020, Minister Terawan had refused permission to seven regions that had requested lockdowns, despite their leaders' sometimes desperate pleas (Kumparan 2020). Anies, for his part, repeatedly called for greater autonomy for local governments to determine their response (Rahman 2020). Other governors and district heads likewise complained publicly about the central government's poor testing and other failings (e.g. Adjie et al. 2020). In some badly hit areas, conflicts erupted over allocation of scarce medical resources between different levels of subnational government – for instance, a conflict between two of Indonesia's best known female politicians, East Java Governor Khofifah Indar Parawansa and Surabaya Mayor Tri Rismaharini (*Jakarta Post* 2020).

Overall, it is possible to find especially in the early months of Indonesia's pandemic response evidence for differing interpretations of the efficacy of decentralization, mirroring long-standing trends in the broader literature. On the one hand, some regional administrations bridled at central-government restrictions, effectively suggesting the government was narrowing the crucial "decision space" that some studies of decentralized public-health governance have found decisive for system effectiveness (e.g. Panda and Thakur 2016). The central government was doing so while pushing much of the burden for crisis-management down to local levels. In this reading, then, Indonesia's problem was really over-centralization. Some local-government leaders, especially in urban areas, were certainly faster to respond to the crisis than the central government (though one finds little evidence of their bypassing the latter), providing further evidence for those who see in decentralization the key to governmental innovation and future prosperity. On the other hand, decentralization enabled poor-quality governance and rent-seeking that shaped poor outcomes in some regions – Papua is an obvious example (IPAC 2020). In short, the central government maintained significant authority, notwithstanding structural decentralization. That balance served to dilute the potential benefits of national-level coordination without offering a more coherent, better-thought-out alternative.

The Philippines presents similar patterns. Decentralization and federalism were cornerstones of Duterte's political agenda (see Rood 2019). Well before the pandemic struck, Duterte, previously mayor of Davao City, drew attention to the excessive centralization of resources in "Imperial Manila" and pitched federalism as, for instance, the only route to peace in restive Mindanao. Given that predilection, COVID-19 presented a test case for building the state's capacity to coordinate among regions while affording them the autonomy to govern based on local circumstances. What the pandemic prompted, however, was further consolidation of authority in the chief executive (Holmes and Hutchcroft 2020). Even more bluntly than in Indonesia, local governments proved more subjects of implementation than agents of innovation – yet the center did not prove up to the task.

Two examples serve to illustrate. First, Duterte signed an executive order in May 2020 encouraging internal-migrant workers to seek employment in their home provinces. He pitched *Balik Probinsya* (Return to the Province)[17] as

---

[17] Available at https://lawphil.net/executive/execord/eo2020/eo_114_2020.html.

a long-term response to the public-health crisis by decongesting the National Capital Region. What could have been a welcome attempt at investing in provincial health, education, livelihoods, and housing instead caused such hassles for local-government officials that the program was suspended after thirty-six days. Among its most vocal critics was Ormoc City Mayor Richard Gomez, who was only advised – via text message – about busloads of repatriates on the day they arrived. Having already successfully closed the city's borders, Gomez had to deal with potentially infected returnees, without corresponding support from the national government for testing and quarantine (Cejas 2020).

Second, central-government disciplinary practices clipped the wings of innovative local governments. In a televised address in March 2020, the president warned local-government officials against deviating from the national taskforce's guidelines. While not named, his target was Pasig City Mayor Vico Sotto, a popular first-term mayor who exempted tricycles (sidecar motorcycles) from the transport ban for the benefit of healthcare workers. The National Bureau of Investigation summoned the mayor for his alleged violation (Gotinga 2020). Though the incident was immediately put to rest, it exemplified the Duterte regime's making examples of "rebel" politicians as a message to other government officials. That said, some mayors had greater success in creating, for instance, "markets on wheels," COVID-19 case-management systems, and localized testing facilities – but still only after bureaucratic turf-wars with the Department of Health (see Presto 2020).

This clearly subpar mix of curbed local authority absent superior central performance in both Indonesia and the Philippines reflects, in part, personal agency – but personal agency may pull in different directions. In Indonesia, President Jokowi's inclination to focus single-mindedly on economic dimensions, as noted earlier – reflecting a broad consensus among Indonesia's ruling elite – was a key factor delaying the response in the critical initial months. The contrast with the Philippines and Duterte, however, is instructive. Though pundits frequently describe both Jokowi and Duterte as populists, the former had a decidedly technocratic bent (Mietzner 2015 provides an astute early take). His response to the pandemic lacked the penal features that came to characterize Duterte's approach. In fact, the strategies the two leaders adopted, however both halting and largely ineffectual, could hardly have been more different, as Duterte pushed lockdown policies adamantly (more on these below) and Jokowi stalled them.

In Indonesia, too, the roster of individuals with personalized authority extends clearly beyond the president; the Philippines' aggressively populist Duterte loomed comparatively larger in setting both tone and policies. At the Indonesian central-government level, of particular note was the role of Health

Minister Terawan – recall his blasé attitude to the new virus in the early months – who came to symbolize to many Indonesians the bumbling nature of the government response. Terawan, the former director of Indonesia's main army hospital, is a controversial figure in Indonesia's medical community. He had won considerable fame among elite Indonesians for a "brain washing" therapy he claimed could prevent stroke, but which neurological experts condemned for lacking supporting evidence; the Indonesian Medical Association found him guilty in 2013 of ethical violations, including "excessive self-promotion" (Rochmyaningsih 2020). Terawan, however, was reputed to have forged close personal ties with Jokowi while treating the president's mother for cancer (she died in March 2020). In reality, problems in the health ministry were systemic as well as personal – it has long had a reputation as one of Indonesia's more cumbersome bureaucracies.

Meanwhile, there is Malaysia, where a highly top-down institutional structure ran up against both political turmoil and unprecedented assertion of local agency. A highly centralized federation and constitutional monarchy, Malaysia has resisted Indonesia- or Philippines-style decentralization and devolution. The Pakatan Harapan (PH) government that came to power in 2018, unseating the Barisan Nasional (BN) coalition dominant since independence in 1957, held out the possibility of restoring local elections and otherwise revisiting power-sharing to at least some extent (Yeoh 2019). That government collapsed in late February 2020 to a palace-facilitated "constitutional coup," just as COVID-19 cases spiked after a super-spreader *Tablighi Jama'at* (Islamic missionary) gathering.[18] The core parties of the BN returned to power as part of a shaky new Perikatan Nasional (PN) alliance. Sapping political will to crack down firmly or to close mosques to stop further spread was not just Islam's place in the public sphere generally but also that Malay-Muslim identity was central to the new coalition: the PN administration was loath to be "accused of hostility to Islam" (Azmil and Por 2021a, 323–324).

Complicating a coordinated pandemic response, though, was not only the fact of leadership in flux but also that parliament remained prorogued for months after the new government took charge, apart from one two-hour sitting mid-May 2020; in January 2021, Prime Minister Muhyiddin Yassin declared a state of emergency and suspended parliament altogether through August. On the positive side, that de-facto insulation may have lent political will to adopt difficult measures. Muhyiddin's government unilaterally announced policy responses, from a protracted lockdown (the Movement Control Order, MCO) to massive

---

[18] Malaysia's Health Ministry estimated 16,000 participants at the gathering, 10 percent attending from abroad (Suraya 2020).

stimulus packages. However, the administration stumbled over policy details, inconsistent implementation, and other gaffes.

Strong assertion of personalistic authority is not the issue in Malaysia. Muhyiddin, then his successor Ismail Sabri Yaakob, remained arguably too weak to allow that. (The PH government's collapse removed the more assertive Mahathir Mohamad as prime minister, but even he had yielded pandemic-management center stage to his popular health minister, Dzulkefly Ahmad.) Rather, in contrast to Indonesia and the Philippines, Malaysia's COVID-19 response arguably laid bare the extent to which the civil service keeps the country afloat, even as missteps strained public confidence in government action. That role hearkened to the salience of a developmental-state legacy – yet one overlaid in Malaysia by, rather than shielded from, politics.

Following PH's fall, Director-General of Health Noor Hisham Abdullah garnered accolades initially for steering the country through pandemic-time political turmoil – *not* new Minister of Health Adham Baba. Indeed, once Adham assumed the latter role, he became "the de facto laughing stock of the nation and a major liability" (Liew 2020a) as (with echoes of his Indonesian counterpart) he recommended that Malaysians drink warm water to flush the coronavirus to the stomach, where acids would kill it before it reached the lungs. Other new ministers likewise blundered – most infamously, the Women, Family, and Community Development Ministry (KPWKM) issued illustrated guidelines encouraging women to avoid nagging, wear makeup, and speak coyly to their stuck-at-home husbands, like cartoon character Doraemon – or made and retracted poor decisions. KPWKM also, for instance, shut down a domestic abuse hotline at the start of the MCO, until pressured to reopen it (Sukhani 2020), and the Minister for Higher Education waffled on whether to require students to remain in university hostels (Wong C. H. 2020, 337). Stiff, unclear, and inconsistent penalties for MCO violations (Malaysiakini 2020a), including apparent double standards for government politicians (Rodzi 2020), incurred public ire. Suggested one commentator, noting "mixed messaging from different ministries and ministers" as Muhyiddin announced yet another nationwide MCO in May 2021, "It often feels like the rules can change at no notice, and businesses and people have to be constantly alert for updates. No announcement can be taken at face value" (Rahman 2021).

Meanwhile, Malaysia diverged from its institutional norm with an unusual assertion of state-government authority. Malaysia's constitution places public health among powers the federal and state governments share concurrently. However, the Local Government Act empowers local councils, which fall under state governments in Malaysia, specifically in matters of disease-prevention, quarantine, and disinfection (Shad Saleem 2020; Yeoh 2020).

When the federal government announced its easing of the initial MCO with just three days' notice in May 2020, nine of Malaysia's thirteen states (both government- and opposition-led), declined to comply at all or in part; others equivocated. They cited still-high case-counts and the need for time to scrutinize federal requirements, consult with local councils, and prepare guidelines. Again when Muhyiddin announced a further-modified Recovery MCO that June, state governments in Penang and Selangor noted that they would review the guidelines, then decide how to proceed.

An obvious driver of this seeming intransigence was the different course of the virus across states and federal territories, but poor communication of federal plans and insufficient effort to build agreement on the best course of action also mattered. Even a PN component-party leader faulted the federal government for not reviewing the proposals with state leaders and securing consensus (Mohd Farhaan 2020). Muhyiddin had likewise failed to inform, let alone consult, state leaders in advance when he gave just over twernty-four hours' notice of the MCO at its initiation in March 2020, leaving southernmost (and PN-led) Johor in particular scrambling to accommodate several hundred thousand Malaysians who commute to Singapore for work. Muhyiddin did convene a meeting of state chief executives the following day, but neglected to invite leaders of opposition-led states. All told, both control and reopening measures demonstrated "an insufficient whole-of-government approach," including inadequate coordination across either ministries or administrative tiers (Liew 2020b), but also a weak center and damaging politicization.

What does this discussion of the relative roles of center versus local, and institutionalization versus personal agency, tell us? One clear conclusion is that in countries where health bureaucracies – and state agencies generally – were relatively well-institutionalized, with clear distribution of authority, and where politics were less personalized and politicized, those bureaucracies could spring into action comparatively swiftly and effectively when the pandemic began. This is the story of Malaysia, as well as Singapore. In both, a competent bureaucracy kicked in to initiate a health response – even if in Malaysia, political upheaval then jostled policymaking and messaging off-course. Indeed, the Malaysian experience throws into stark relief an underlying feature of Malaysian politics: amid sometimes tumultuous party politics and endemic communalized rent-seeking, an empowered civil service extends a strong state role in development. In Vietnam, too, "long-standing efforts to professionalize the administrative state," including by simultaneously "strengthening coordination with lower administrative levels and effectively utilizing centralized resources" allowed quick, effective containment measures (Nguyen and Malesky 2020). However, how deeply partisan considerations permeate in

Malaysia allowed rent-seeking and patronage politicking to temper bureaucratic decision-making (see Washida 2019).

In contrast, in Indonesia and the Philippines, where political institutions are less robust, undermined by patronage-seeking legislators and increasingly populist executives, political leaders' decisions had much greater import, precluding both bureaucratic and local-government autonomy. To be sure, lower state capacity in both cases exacerbated these states' flimsier health responses. However, what these divergent approaches really demonstrate is how much personal politics and incomplete devolution matter in places where institutions remain relatively weak – and how much space personalization and hazy chains of accountability allow for decisions to be guided less by epidemiological expertise than by leaders' priorities, beliefs, and habitual strategic repertoires. These considerations lead us to our third dimension, of the political climate more broadly.

State–Society Relations

It is hardly surprising that the pandemic tested the patience of citizens in their leaders and vice-versa. Not even in the best of times is concordance on values and priorities assured between state and society, even at the local level. Indeed, an important (negative) outcome, across the region, was acceleration or amplification of illiberalization (including Malaysia's early-pandemic democratic reversal). As noted earlier, regime type proved an inconsistent predictor of the effectiveness of a state's response, yet causality could still run in the other direction: the pandemic shaped regimes.

Democratic backsliding has long been a concern in most of Southeast Asia, apart from in those states that make no pretense of liberalism in the first place. While scholars differ on how to characterize this process and the factors that erode the quality of democratic institutions and practices (see Mietzner 2021), that a pandemic might exacerbate this trend is incontrovertible. The threat of contagion, in fact, created an enabling environment for regimes region-wide to operate with enhanced or emergency powers – though populations proved discriminating in the extent to which they tolerate different measures (Aspinall et al. 2021). Unsurprisingly, much of the literature on state responses to COVID-19 in Southeast Asia focuses on detailing the rollback of democratic processes. Four aspects of that rollback proved most salient, and fed into a broader dialectic between framing the pandemic as more a matter of security, mandating state control of presumed-wayward citizens, or of public health, in which state and society collaborate to pull through.

First and foremost, executive power concentrated to enable swift decisions. The pandemic offered opportunities to pass new legislation, issue executive orders, and waive ordinary procedural checks without clear limits on when to lift expanded state power. Exhibit A is Malaysia's declaration of emergency when cases surged in January 2021: suspending parliament conveniently enabled the embattled prime minister to stave off a likely vote of no confidence. Meanwhile, the Philippines' Congress granted President Rodrigo Duterte sweeping emergency powers, including over local-government operations, private health services, and the national budget (Hapal 2021, 230).

Second, the pandemic justified an increased role for state security forces to enforce lockdown rules. Ex-generals staffed the Philippines' policymaking Inter-Agency Taskforce on Emerging Infectious Diseases – "the oddest task force to fight the pandemic, a squad full of soldiers without a single epidemiologist" (Makabenta 2020) – and police and military spearheaded the nation's pandemic response. Soldiers roamed the streets of Manila and Cebu, monitored highways and checkpoints, and exhorted residents via loudspeaker trucks to stay home (Hall 2022). These operations gave the regime cover, too, to intensify an ongoing counter-insurgency operation by profiling volunteer groups organizing community pantries and investigating their links to the Communist Party of the Philippines, without cause (Santos 2021). Similarly, in Thailand, an "Army Delivery" initiative embedded soldiers within social activities, boosting their capacity to surveil citizens (Piyapong and Pobsook 2020, 362).

Third, most Southeast Asian states tightened media controls to curb pandemic-related disinformation, implementing versions of anti-"fake news" legislation, with wider effects. Observers warned that laws against disinformation had been weaponized to target members of opposition political parties and activist groups. Human Rights Watch (2020), for example, documented thirty cases of arbitrary arrest in Cambodia in a span of four weeks. The regime accused members of the dissolved Cambodian National Rescue Party and other activists of "distributing information that could scare the public" or cause unrest and "negatively impact national security" under the state's national emergency law. In neighboring Thailand, Prime Minister Prayuth Chan-o-cha's regime launched Anti-Fake News Centers to monitor misleading online content – and considered criticisms of the state's handling of the outbreak as "misleading" and therefore punishable (see Sochua 2020). The pandemic helped to vindicate, too, Singapore's then-recently passed, and still controversial, Protection from Online Falsehoods and Manipulation Act (POFMA), pressing even platforms such as Facebook into compliance (Mahtani 2020). Malaysia tightened access to certain COVID-19-related information while penalizing critics (Crispin 2020).

Lastly, lockdown orders across the region effectively suspended civil liberties, particularly by banning even small-scale gatherings to avert the spread of the virus, and undermined social and economic rights. The Philippines' Duterte went a step further following a protest in Manila among urban-poor communities aggrieved by the government's failure to provide food aid or cash allowances after two weeks' confinement. Should they encounter anyone creating "trouble" during the lockdown, he ordered, the military should "shoot them dead" (Tomacruz 2020). Duterte's over-the-top stance illustrates the extent to which his government not only suspended freedom of assembly but, in line with his broader securitizing impulse (as noted earlier), styled it as a threat to national security. Meanwhile, that the pandemic did not stop mass anti-regime protests in Myanmar, and only temporarily paused them in Thailand (Thanthong-Knight 2021), reflects not a more lax approach but simply the extent to which protesters ignored the threat of contagion or penalty to demonstrate against military regimes in both states (Peter 2021).

These questions of authority and approach shape all aspects of governance, but had especially trenchant effects for how governments in the region framed the pandemic, and citizens, in turn, responded. Indeed, even in the region's high-performing developmental states, well-trained obeisance entwined inextricably with tightened curbs. Yet since efforts to evade the rules (a public-health twist on rent-seeking) could have devastating effects, sufficient confidence in the state to deliver positive, public-serving outcomes that citizens comply instead of pushing back is helpful. A public-health frame evokes and requires a different public reaction than a public-security frame, but requires a level of technical competency and public trust to enact.

Such framing may be read in part from how policies played out on the ground: what encouraged or obliged citizens to comply with public-health directives, and which agencies' budgets and ambits expanded amid the pandemic? Most obviously, to what extent could governments count on voluntary compliance from citizens who trusted their judgment, rather than coerce compliance through stepped-up reliance on security agencies? Did trained health professionals have the authority and credibility to take charge of public-health outreach and messaging? The poles of this continuum are especially revealing: a clearly defined public-health frame, with Singapore as exemplar, and a similarly stark public-security frame in Duterte's Philippines – yet even these polar cases vacillated between modes. Focusing on such framing, however, highlights the extent to which regime type itself matters less than the sources of legitimacy on which states rely in an emergency. Where past abuses, from corruption to repression to exclusionary particularism, might lead citizens to doubt authorities' motives, those leaders could not simply wipe clean their slates.

Singapore's response began squarely at the public-health pole, although it veered off-course with regard to migrant workers as events developed. Early on,

Singapore's government established a framework for clear, consistent communication of guidelines and data.[19] Those efforts built trust, facilitated effective contact-tracing, and fostered buy-in with new rules. Official communications circulated online via social media such as WhatsApp, traditional platforms, and creative approaches such as cartoons,[20] and remained straightforward, authoritative, and frequent. A well-pitched televised address by the prime minister, for instance, restored calm when the first bout of rising cases sparked panic-buying and anxiety, validating the government's turn toward clear, rational explanation (Fisher 2020; Li and Tan 2020).

The Singapore government's response remained careful and calibrated. Its strategy initially "eschewed strict movement control, favoring instead contact tracing and isolation of a few in order to maintain freedom of movement for the many" (Neo and Lee 2020). The Ministry of Health and other government agencies sought to secure compliance for the public good, without coercion. Existing laws – the Infectious Diseases Act (fortified during the SARS epidemic) and the Immigration Act – structured the government's preliminary response, soon supplemented by a COVID-19 (Temporary Measures) Act (CTMA) that passed in a single day as a partial lockdown, or "circuit-breaker," began. It was that law and associated regulations that stipulated permitted and proscribed activities as well as penalties for violations.

Public health remained central to how the state framed pandemic-management, at least among Singaporeans and permanent residents. The CTMA did have teeth, however. Individuals were to stay home except for specific purposes (e.g. essential work or purchasing necessities) or for exercise, and were to maintain safe distance in nearly all circumstances. Penalties for violations were steep: up to SGD10,000 (USD7,450) and/or six months' prison, and worse for repeat offenders. Officers issued only warnings for the first few days, then switched to on-the-spot SGD300 (USD225) fines. Violating leave-of-absence or stay-home notice rules (under the Infectious Diseases Act) could result in revocation of a work pass or cancellation of permanent-resident status or a Singapore citizen's passport (Neo and Lee 2020). Even so, officials were at pains to explain that their contact-tracing smartphone app, TraceTogether, would safeguard privacy, from

---

[19] Vietnam, too, focused on curbing infection rates by changing personal behavior, via campaigns that resonated with citizens' worldviews and habits, relying heavily on early, prolific, and informative articles, circulated over social media. As in Singapore, "although the state has the tools to control the flow and content of information," it opted "to be transparent in this case," complementing contact-tracing, quarantine, and other measures, and recognizing the need for "top-down communication" to motivate "bottom-up engagement" (Nguyen and Ho 2020, 2–4).

[20] One flop: the "Virus Vanguard" – superheroes Dr. Disinfector, Fake News Buster, MAWA [Must Always Walk Alone] Man, Circuit Breaker, and Care-leh Dee – were roundly panned and promptly retracted.

both government agents and potential hackers – though sceptics noted its alignment with Singapore's inherently privacy-comprising "Smart Nation" strategy of tracking "E3A: Everyone, Everything, Everywhere, All the Time" (Haines and Stevens 2020).

Where this approach took a twist was, again, in the state's treatment of dormitory-resident foreign workers – whose living as well as working conditions Singapore's state-structured development planning strictly regulates. They were subject to complete lockdown, confined indoors in infection-conducive overcrowded rooms, in the name of protecting Singaporeans, regardless of the obvious risks to those workers' own health. A strategy centered on public health for citizens and permanent residents came to foreground coercive containment – security – among the low-wage foreign labor on whom Singapore's growth model significantly rests. The government soon committed to improving foreign workers' housing density and living conditions long term, and to building new dormitories closer to residential areas, to discourage "NIMBY" attitudes (Today 2020). But the aim still seemed more to safeguard citizens from future worker-transmitted disease than to improve those workers' welfare as an end in itself, as by approaching them as rightful targets of public-health interventions rather than as vectors to be controlled (see Han 2020b).

At the other end of the spectrum lies the Philippines. That the Philippines' COVID-19 story unfolded against the backdrop of an increasingly illiberal regime supports the premise that authoritarianism per se is no public-health panacea. In 2016, Rodrigo Duterte won the presidency by a wide margin; his party's sweep of Senate elections in 2019, a postwar first, further consolidated his mandate. Exemplifying Duterte's approach was his notorious war against drugs, which combined dehumanizing rhetoric with deputizing police to enforce community-level anti-drug operations, resulting in tens of thousands of deaths (Coronel et al. 2019). That securitizing, brute-force ethos infused his administration's response to COVID-19. After initial complacency, as local transmission increased in March 2020, Duterte placed the entire country under a state of public-health emergency. After months of one of the world's longest and strictest lockdowns, the Philippines nevertheless had the highest number of COVID-19 cases in Southeast Asia, with capital-city Manila as epicenter.

While the Philippines, like Indonesia, has a history of a politically engaged military, prior leaders have sought to change course. In 2014, for example, then-President Benigno Aquino created a Task Force on Emerging Infectious Diseases to respond to threats of SARS and MERS, as well as recurring diseases such as leptospirosis and meningococcemia. Its leaders are civilians, from departments including Health, Interior and Local Government, Labor and

Employment, and Transportation and Communications (Porcalla 2014). But institutions under the Duterte regime – even in normal times – took on a distinctly militaristic character.

Duterte's approach reflected his idealized view of the armed forces as efficient and obedient. As presidential spokesperson Salvador Panelo described, "They are not embroiled in bureaucratic rigmaroles. They abhor useless debates, they are silent workers, not voracious talkers. ... They get things done."[21] Leading Duterte's National Taskforce on COVID-19 were former military generals who also served in the Cabinet, chaired by Defense Chief Delfin Lorenzana (who also headed Duterte's National Disaster Risk Reduction and Management Council), with Secretary of the Interior Eduardo Año as vice chair. Also on the taskforce were the national security adviser and ministers of Social Welfare and Information, Communications, and Technology – all of them retired from military service.

The apparatus of state violence was "overtly visible" in enforcing the government's COVID-19 response (Suzuki 2020). "I am just asking for your discipline," Duterte insisted in April 2020 – but should people break the rules, it "will be like martial law" (Dancel 2020). For many Filipinos, however, "discipline" was not a viable option: staying home meant dying of hunger. The first month of lockdown saw 30,000 violators arrested, a figure that far exceeded the number of people tested for the virus. Human rights groups warned of uneven, and, in many cases, abusive, treatment of lockdown violators. Some were confined to dog cages; others were beaten up or humiliated by being made "to kiss, dance, or do push-ups" while being streamed on social media (Thoreson 2020). Meanwhile, police arrested Pride March and Anti-Terror Bill protesters without warrants, even though they followed rules on social distancing, and a journalist was arrested for removing his mask to drink water. The director of field operations for the United Nations' human rights office faulted the "police and other security forces" for "using excessive and sometimes deadly force to enforce lockdowns and curfews" (Aspinwall 2020). The mass detention of violators further increased contagion risks. As in Malaysia, where raids against refugees and undocumented migrant workers continued through the pandemic, congested prisons and jails became coronavirus hotspots. Even as outcomes made plain its inadequacy, centrally directed securitization remained the Philippines' default response.

Other states in the region fell between these poles. Indonesia inclined toward the Philippines, though less strongly securitized: far from insulated from

---

[21] Press statement, March 27, 2020, https://pcoo.gov.ph/OPS-content/on-the-raison-d-etre-on-the-presidents-appointment-of-ex-military-men-to-lead-the-implementation-of-the-national-policy-against-covid-19/.

politics, Jokowi's administration shied away from unpopular measures, however warranted. As discussed earlier, the instincts of national leaders – the president as well as top security officials – from the start were to downplay the seriousness of the crisis and to avoid harshly restrictive counter-measures. That said, the Indonesian military and police played prominent roles in crisis-management and enforcing regulations, both at the central level and in the regions, albeit lacking so notably harsh or disciplinary an approach as in the Philippines. In mid-April 2020, for instance, the national police, with remarkable precision, said they and the military had broken up 205,502 mass gatherings over the preceding month (Halim 2020). The following month, Jokowi announced that 340,000 police and military officers would help to enforce social restrictions associated with his "new normal" framework (Lumanauw et al. 2020).

Health Minister (and retired lieutenant general) Terawan Agus Putranto's prominence was telling: his own army pedigree highlighted the degree to which Jokowi came to rely on the military as the public face of his pandemic response and, to an extent, for its organization. Military officers took on key roles, leaning into the military's territorial command structure, and extending to appointing even active military and police officials as interim regional leaders (Sambhi 2021; *Jakarta Globe* 2022). For instance, the head of the main COVID-19 task force was a lieutenant general and former special forces commander, Doni Murtado. According to Laksmana and Taufika (2020), at least twenty-one retired and active duty officers were "directly involved in the decision-making process of the various mitigation efforts at the national level," while at the "local level, hundreds of TNI [army] officers are assigned as deputy chiefs of local COVID-19 task forces." They stress that the military did not dominate, but played a significant role in, mitigation efforts nationwide. A large part of the health budget for the COVID-19 response was even channeled through the military: in April 2020, the national parliament approved a 3.2 trillion rupiah (USD217 million) funding boost to the institution to support its COVID-19 efforts (Bisnis.com 2020).

By giving the military such a prominent role, Jokowi followed a pattern set early in his presidency. Even more than his predecessor, former general Susilo Bambang Yudhoyono, he had relied increasingly on senior retired military and police officers to fill important cabinet posts, and, critically, re-engaged the military in development and nation-building projects in fields ranging from disaster-management to agricultural distribution (on the latter: Graham 2020). In doing so, Jokowi built on a critical institutional legacy. For decades, especially during the authoritarian "New Order" regime of President Suharto (1966–1998) the military sustained a virtual parallel government, providing it with the institutional memory, apparatus, and interest to slot relatively easily back into governance roles in the contemporary period. Largely as a result of that legacy, the military and its leaders have a reputation among elite and ordinary Indonesians alike as among Indonesia's more effective institutions, largely accounting for the appeal of a militarized approach for Jokowi – and highlighting the extent to which historical-institutional legacies mold the policy landscape. That said, no matter the degree to which the military benefited from their enhanced public profile and budgets, the main burden of the national response inevitably fell on the shoulders of health, welfare, and civil-administration officers at the local level, raising the complex issues regarding the division between national and local authority noted earlier.

Signs also emerged during the pandemic of the wider creeping autocratization that had marked Indonesia for much of the last decade. For example, in early April 2020, the Chief of National Police circulated a telegram instructing officers to take action against persons insulting the president or other officials (Briantika 2020). The police also stepped up electronic surveillance efforts, charging fifty-one persons just by the end of March 2020 for circulating hoaxes about the coronavirus (Zhacky 2020). Various instances arose during the pandemic of police harassment of government critics, while the national government tried to push several laws with repressive features through parliament.

At the same time, public-health experts faulted lax enforcement of travel and capacity restrictions more even than a contagious new strain for a mid-2021 surge. Explained a virologist from Bali's Udayana University, "the Delta variant is being used as a scapegoat because of the government's incapacity to control the pandemic" (Al Jazeera 2021). Moreover, the harshest restrictions tended to be enacted at the micro-level, by villages and neighborhoods engaging in forms of grassroots policing and blocking outsiders' access, building on traditions of community-level vigilantism directed against crime and threats to public order (see Jaffrey 2019). Nor was the Indonesian response, on the whole, marked by stigmatization of particular groups as vectors of infection, as occurred with migrant workers in Singapore (and Malaysia, explored later in this section). Itself a major labor exporter, Indonesia lacks a significant population of migrant workers; stigmatization was instead widely distributed. Virtually anyone who contracted COVID-19 risked being socially ostracized – there were even reports of villages' refusing entry to mourners who wished to bury their dead.

These developments continued Indonesia's slow slide toward illiberalism; they did not mark a dramatic break with trends apparent throughout Jokowi's presidency, including both gradual political resurrection of the security apparatus and its post-Suharto pattern of all-inclusive governing coalitions. National and subnational or local governments were often greatly concerned about taking steps that key societal constituencies would see as harsh or discriminatory.

In particular, they hesitated significantly in limiting religious activities for fear of backlash from Muslim mass organizations, an important political base for multiple parties. (Illiberal Islamic groups specifically also wielded political influence.) Although the government did enact and enforce restrictions in some areas, in others, decisions undermined social-distancing efforts – as when the East Java provincial government allowed mass prayers in the lead-up to Idulfitri in 2020, effectively undermining efforts by Surabaya's city government to limit mass gatherings (Hasani 2020). In such respects, the broadly coalitional nature of Indonesia's democratic politics and lack of an insulated decision-making apparatus undermined not only either technocratic direction *or* Philippine-populist-style securitization but also effectiveness.

For its part, Malaysia inclined toward the public-health pole, although pandemic-control efforts saw a clear uptick in illiberal policing and surveillance. Especially important to Malaysia's performance was the political meltdown just as the pandemic took off – especially since the government that collapsed was the first since independence *not* helmed by the Barisan Nasional. Massive rent-seeking had so undermined popular confidence that the coalition had lost the 2018 elections. In the unprecedented position of being without its typically dominant central government two years later, Malaysia could not draw upon the sort of authoritative decision-making and public trust that its substantially developmentalist record might otherwise have fostered. That politicians then milked aid efforts for partisan gain, in line with endemic credit-claiming (Weiss 2020, 127–131), reinforced how politicized pandemic-management was. For instance, the National Welfare Foundation, under the Women, Family, and Community Development Ministry, provided food aid for affected households: 1,000 packs per constituency, each worth MYR100 (about USD24). Opposition members of parliament (MPs) raised concerns that families on lists they had given the Social Welfare Department had received nothing, that government-party representatives were distributing aid-packs in opposition constituencies, or that police obstructed opposition MPs who circulated during the MCO period to distribute aid (Bersih 2020b; *Malaysiakini* 2020b and 2020c; Ngu 2021). Legislators from across parties also pasted their own names and faces on handouts such as rice and hand-sanitizer to claim personal credit (Bersih 2020a).

Less on-brand for Malaysia was the entry of security forces into government functions. As many as 7,500 troops from across the armed forces joined police in enforcing the initial MCO. They focused on "high-risk areas" like markets and hospitals, to ensure compliance with regulations (Rahmat 2020). Within three months, security personnel had arrested over 6,000 for flouting MCO rules (Ainaa 2020). Police and military roadblocks also screened for immigration offenses, and police rather than public-health workers monitored compliance with home quarantine and other procedures (Camoens 2020).

But where public-health efforts gave way most sharply to securitization was with migrants – albeit with a rather different root and logic than in Singapore. Rising xenophobia toward migrant workers and refugees, particularly Rohingya – the government turned away boatloads during the MCO, although previously comparatively accepting of these fellow-Muslims[22] – exacerbated an already-bad situation, with far-reaching public-health implications. For instance, the majority of attendees at the aforementioned mass religious gathering who evaded post-hoc state calls to appear for screening were Rohingya asylum-seekers, afraid to approach authorities (Daniel 2020).

Not only did crowding in vehicles and immigration centers – known sites for outbreaks – increase the risk of contagion, but the effort directly contravened prior policy. Claimed Defense Minister Ismail Sabri in March 2020, "We won't focus on their documents but rather on whether they are positive with Covid-19"; in a late April reversal, he announced that undocumented individuals found in "red zones" still under an "enhanced MCO" would be transported to detention centers or special prisons (Sukumaran and Jaipragas 2020). A month later, he elaborated: undocumented migrants had no right to be in Malaysia, and might "spread the virus to innocent people" (Bernama 2020). Within hours of the government's announcing the impending phase-out of the first MCO, civil defense, police, and immigration forces raided red-zone low-cost apartment buildings, packing detainees, including refugees and children, into lorries bound for the immigration depot. Malaysia presumably feared a Singapore-style outbreak among migrant workers: these buildings housed thousands, densely packed, most of them migrants (Sukumaran and Jaipragas 2020). All told, the government arrested at least 2,000 foreigners in a series of raids in May 2020, including probably around 800 Rohingya asylum-seekers.[23] Those testing negative for COVID-19 faced deportation; those testing positive were sent to quarantine centers first for treatment. The cycle repeated in June 2021, as different ministers either urged undocumented workers to come forward for vaccination, promising their safety, or vowed to lock them up (Anand 2021).

The approach, critics noted, was at odds with public-health objectives, since likely to push even clearly sick migrants into hiding – nine of those detained in

---

[22] Malaysia deported over 1,000 migrants to Myanmar, notwithstanding a court injunction, in February 2021; their ranks included other ethnic minorities at risk of persecution in Myanmar, but not, Malaysian authorities clarified, Rohingya (BBC 2021).

[23] Over 100,000 Rohingya live in Malaysia, however tenuous their status, having previously been more tolerated. COVID-19 aside, for asylum-seekers to return to Myanmar or elsewhere, of course, could prove devastating.

the initial raids, for instance, fled from a quarantine center, as did at least 145 workers at a construction site where colleagues had tested positive. And immigration detention-center cases could readily wreak havoc there, as well as filtering outside (Ding 2020).[24] An Al Jazeera exposé on the plight of undocumented migrant workers in Malaysia, following the raids, led Malaysian police to investigate whether the broadcaster may have violated sedition, defamation, or media laws (and to deport a Bangladeshi worker interviewed in the documentary) – part of a larger crackdown on the press and publishing (Al Jazeera 2020). Attacks on refugee-rights activists surged online, too, and the government threatened legal action against advocacy groups, even as a UN official cautioned that the "hate campaign" undermined COVID-control efforts (Ananthalakshmi and Latiff 2020).

Thailand, too, veered between approaches. Overall, the government, like Singapore's, defaulted to clear explanation and to well-organized transmission of containment plans and information between central-government policymakers and regional and local policy-implementers. Thai citizens largely complied with quarantine and other rules, understanding why they were needed (Sirisak et al. 2021). Coordinated deployment of village health volunteers further ensured hyper-local, responsive outreach (e.g. Amporn and Vithaya 2021). Nevertheless, framing COVID-19 explicitly as a nontraditional, existential security threat, Prime Minister Prayuth announced a state of emergency over television in late March "as if he had staged another coup to seize power," applying a law never before exercised for other than military operations, and "prefer[ring] exercising special executive powers to following normal parliamentary processes" or working within "regular laws" (Supalak 2020, 5, 7). Here, too, a public-health response vied with a securitizing impulse built on habits of illiberal governance – in this case of working not through the bureaucracy but through the executive and military.

In short, regional experience points both to the insistent pull of the path well-traveled – the historical-institutional roots of present policies – and to how branching and brambly those paths may be. Significant variation emerged in the way dueling impulses and options played out, notwithstanding a common theme of democratic decline, alongside significant ambiguity in the extent to which securitization of pandemic responses bled into a broader remaking of state–society relations. In both Malaysia and Singapore, the striking trend was for securitization of vulnerable migrants, whom these governments identified as a major source of contagion (and, especially in Singapore, as a distressing blight

---

[24] Meanwhile, an estimated 80 percent of refugees who had (illegal) jobs prior to the MCO lost them; rising unemployment led employers to hire Malaysians, instead.

on their record of pandemic-management success). Yet countervailing pressures encouraged greater transparency and openness, as well. In the Philippines and Thailand, by contrast, securitization targeted the citizenry as a whole. Still, particularly in the former, the state's capacity to enforce compliance with public-health measures was limited. Philippine citizens complied visibly, as by wearing masks, to avoid punishment, even as living conditions and subsistence requirements made skirting rules otherwise inevitable – and the Thai government's response cannot be fully disentangled from its crackdown on political protests. Indonesia, as the foregoing discussion suggests, is an intermediate case, evincing both a reflexive turn toward the military and a reluctance to overdo coercion. (Section 4 explores the region's similarly mottled record on socio-economic rights specifically, especially as embodied in welfare-state safety-nets.)

Importantly, these trends occurred in a context that was propitious for an at-least temporary winding-back of civil rights: in surveys Gallup conducted in April 2020, amid lockdowns and other measures, the statement, "I am willing to sacrifice some of my human rights if it helps prevent the spread of the virus," elicited 81 percent approval in Malaysia, 83 percent in Indonesia, 86 percent in the Philippines, and 92 percent in Thailand.[25] It is striking, however, that these responses did not differ dramatically from those of respondents in Europe; the real outliers were the United States, where 68 percent agreed with the statement, and Japan, where only 40 percent did so. Intriguingly, however, the same survey found that only small minorities in Indonesia (15 percent), the Philippines (18 percent), and Thailand (20 percent) agreed, "Democracy is not effective in such a crisis" – whereas in Malaysia, the figure was much higher, at 43 percent, perhaps reflecting popular frustration with government instability *or* willingness to trust state management. Supporting the former interpretation: as democracy deteriorated in Malaysia, public support for the government's handling of the crisis plunged, from consistently above 90 percent through late September 2020, to a nadir of 29 percent in mid-July 2021, as the initial PN administration unraveled. Levels fluctuated in other Southeast Asian states for which data are available (Indonesia, Philippines, Singapore, Vietnam), but less dramatically. Notably, support remained consistently lowest in the Philippines and Indonesia and highest in Vietnam and Singapore – the two states with the strongest record of state-led management, and, arguably, the least need or predilection to allow political palatability to guide decision-making.[26]

---

[25] The survey excluded the rest of Southeast Asia. COVID19 Wave2: Tables, https://impetus-research.com/wp-content/uploads/2020/01/GIA_COVID19_Snap%20Poll_W2_ALL_QQ_TABLES-V8.PDF.

[26] YouGov COVID-19 tracker: government handling, https://today.yougov.com/topics/international/articles-reports/2020/03/17/perception-government-handling-covid-19 (accessed August 20, 2024).

4 Implications and Conclusions

How, and how well, states managed the COVID-19 crisis matters not only for the pace and depth of public-health and economic recovery but also in disentangling analytically the state from politics. This inquiry carries implications for our understanding of what damage democratic decline can (and cannot) do and for updating the literature on developmental statehood, especially in light of postindustrial economic restructuring. It is helpful, too, for the insight it offers into how states may navigate other existential crises of our time, such as climate change. It is thus worth taking stock of what we have learned and what it means by exploring these dimensions, including what one might expect as the inevitable next iteration gains steam. I aim to present not a definitive last word on crisis governance but a plausible, evidence-backed hypothesis: attributes that made the developmental-state model effective for Asian industrialization may be similarly useful for navigating a pandemic and its economic fallout, but real distribution of authority cannot be read from structure (and matters to how policymaking plays out). Moreover, given cover to default toward illiberalism, states already listing that direction might speed their drift, however counterproductive. In short, the range of ideological premises these cases present and the variation in their economic and welfare responses to the crisis allow consideration not just of what is likely most effective but also, à la Gourevitch (1986), the extent to which hard times induce readjustment, given what tools a given state *can* reasonably command or citizens might expect states to wield.

Managing the Economy: "Developmentalism" Diffused?

To recap, effective pandemic governance benefits from a state's ability to marshal not just resources but also capacity across sectors – in this case, health care, but also manufacturing, financial services, and other domains essential to biotech innovation and speedier economic recovery. Yet as these cases also indicate, that capacity alone is insufficient. Technocratic management, insulated from partisan politicking and rent-seeking, is helpful in recognizing problems and implementing solutions, but a specifically coercive variant may not secure the sort of popular buy-in most germane in a pandemic or may buckle under pressure. Compliance with, for instance, negotiated wage policies or industrial plans is more straightforward and limited in scope. Ensuring all residents follow public-health mandates is particularly challenging, given the pervasive, disabling behavioral changes required, and how difficult these are to monitor (not to mention the fact that enforcement itself steps up risks for officials involved).

Authoritarian predilections may align with developmental statehood, but these categories only partly coincide. The key issue in this context seems more trust in the government's record and probity than the simple scope of its authority to oblige compliance. Hence, for instance, Singapore's PAP could win an election mid-pandemic (albeit with reduced margins of victory), whereas the Malaysian and Thai regimes had cause to fear, and used the pandemic as premise to suppress regime-threatening blowback. In Malaysia, in particular, that worry precluded optimal policy development. Thailand's military-backed ruling Palang Pracharat Party (PPRP) worked closely with major Thai conglomerates and could, through public–private partnerships, jumpstart economic sectors. Yet those companies shared a political motive with the government: they helped fund both protests "that paved the way for the coup" and PPRP's election campaign, and aimed "to displace the populist initiatives associated with [rival] Thaksin [Shinawatra] while winning over his provincial voters" (ICG 2020, 7). Resulting initiatives would be liable to be read as partisan. In short, although they can develop by other paths, genuinely durable trust and credibility may be a legacy and extension of political insulation of bureaucratic decision-making in pursuit of progress and "performance legitimacy," as under developmental-state structures.

Regardless, the fact even of having once been a full-fledged developmental state does not itself ensure that a regime retains capacity to resurrect those habits effectively in a crisis, institutional legacies notwithstanding, nor that they will be fully sufficient. Certain aspects of that legacy may be more germane than others – and may extend to those Asian NICs, like Malaysia or Thailand, that never fully met developmental-state criteria. Political drift and economic restructuring (especially toward service industries and the "gig economy"), too, may erode these paths, including intervening democratization, or at least inculcation of greater popular expectations of voice, transparency, and accountability. The latter shift has tended to diminish bureaucratic facility (Beeson 2010, 279).

Indeed, as Bäck and Hadenius (2008, 1–2) demonstrate, "The world has become more democratic, but the administrative capacity of states appears to have diminished"; it is only in the most strongly democratic states that administrative quality increases apace.[27] Only-partly democratized states perform worse than authoritarian ones, they find, because "steering and control" shift over the course of democratic transition from top-down to bottom-up as societal forces accumulate resources and strength. That pattern offers useful insight into why the governments of Singapore, Thailand, and Vietnam were able swing into effective action in ways less feasible in Indonesia, the Philippines, or Malaysia. Backsliding notwithstanding, pressures of accountability and expectations of

---

[27] Yet nor does political liberalism guarantee positive developmental outcomes. The (pre-Duterte) Philippines had, for instance, both "arguably the most vibrant civil society in Southeast Asia" and "one of the most appalling environmental records" (Beeson 2010, 281).

voice in the latter states meant coordination and resources were *not* so fully "controlled within one and the same decision making arena" as under centralized control from above. Even so, these polities lacked the sort of constructive "dialogue and cooperation" between state and societal actors that can elevate strongly democratic states' administrative capacity above that of authoritarian counterparts (Bäck and Hadenius 2008, 14–16).[28]

As is evident in retrospect, the economic fallout proved arguably at least as devastating and enduring as the public-health emergency. Not only was regime type a similarly poor predictor of these policy responses, but the depth and unpredictability of crisis scrambled all the usual roadmaps. It is this dimension that manifests especially clearly both the salience and insufficiency of institutional history. Developmental-state experience should prime states for well-targeted, centrally administered aid; for a focus structured around roles in production chains (e.g., favoring useful manufacturers and welfare support to keep workers productive and quiescent); and for top-down decision-making little buffeted by political winds.

In the decades preceding the pandemic, states across the region had introduced important new social-protection programs, including for healthcare, bolstering socioeconomic rights. Indonesia's introduction of a new, redistributive national health-insurance program in the wake of the Asian financial crisis (AFC), amid post-Suharto democratization (Aspinall 2014), is a prime example of that recalibration of state–society relations – and, on face, squarely akin to East Asian transitions to developmental welfare states (Kwon 2007). But the initiative also clarifies how politicized, partial, and captured such policymaking may remain, notwithstanding the breadth of participation reforms entail (Aspinall 2014), and how still mired in clientelist relationships that retard a more formalized, programmatic turn (Yuda and Kühner 2023). The pandemic saw movement toward further welfare-state development, but less firmly or enduringly than the scope of the crisis and the precarity it laid bare might suggest. Across the region's middle-income capitalist states, some extent of crisis-precipitated elevation of technocrats and progressives proved insufficient to rebalance or reconfigure power substantially or to overcome Southeast Asian social-protection systems' productivist conservativism more than temporarily (Rosser and Murphy 2023, 2, 20–25).

In practice, while COVID-19 relief packages proliferated throughout the region, states tossed so many darts at the recovery target that patterns are hard to discern. All states offered some form of direct payments or grants, but

---

[28] For a cognate take on Hong Kong, where unresponsive, opaque, paternalistic governance sapped community trust and impeded the SARS response: Hayllar 2007.

approaches varied otherwise.[29] One can sketch an overall continuum – nowhere a dichotomy – in economic interventions, from assuming a state-led to a market-led recovery, as well as in how programmatic or partisan interventions were. Measures pursued embodied political logics, from who was included or left out, to expectations of state responsibility for popular welfare. Nor did emergency-relief measures serve to codify new economic rights or entitlements, even to the extent that they acknowledged the wide gaps in the current system.

Signaling the contingency of economic crisis-management: within Southeast Asia, only in Singapore and the Philippines did COVID-19 relief come through legislative enactment rather than by decree (UNODC [2020]), however still-opaque the policy process. Elsewhere, executive fiat shut the legislature out entirely. For instance, Thailand's emergency decree on COVID-19 "does not mention the Parliament or the exercise of Parliamentary oversight" and allowed for yet greater expansion of executive power (UNODC [2020]). In the Philippines, too, the Bayanihan Act authorized President Duterte to "reallocate, realign, and reprogram" a sum amounting to 63 percent of the 2020 national budget for pandemic-response, including "social amelioration" programs for the poor and vulnerable (Gudmalin et al. 2021, 2), and to "temporarily take over or direct the operations" of public utilities and private health or other facilities in the "public interest." The president did report weekly to a Congressional oversight committee, however, allowing some accountability for his deployment of emergency funds (UNODC [2020]).

A brief sketch of the economic-support approaches the illustrative cases of Singapore, Malaysia, and Indonesia adopted, and via what political processes, clarifies the mix of decisions and outcomes involved. I start with Singapore, where a developmentalist legacy, including centralized authority, is inescapably germane. The state controls a substantial share of the economy (Chua 2017), giving it an outsize stake in, and capacity to shape, its recovery. All told, Singapore's economy came through reasonably well: although real GDP contracted by 5.4 percent in 2020, it rebounded to a year-on-year 1.3 percent growth rate by first-quarter 2021 ... alas, just in time for yet another lockdown midyear (IMF 2021).

Yet the character of pandemic relief, if less its genesis, entailed some shift from common practice, even there. Singapore's PAP government has long eschewed a "welfare" frame; recall Singapore's lesser embrace than its East Asian counterparts of "inclusive welfare-developmentalism" (Kwon 2007). The pandemic challenged the state's usual preference for benefits based on employment and paying-in (Lim 2020), or for "a trickle-down model of help

---

[29] See UNODC [2020] for a list.

premised on protecting businesses" (Teo and Ng 2020), nudging it toward developmentalist welfare statism. The role of low-paid essential workers, including gig-economy workers, in the pandemic response forced recalibration. Amid strikingly high income inequality, a significant share of Singaporeans already experienced precarity, including many of the cleaners, delivery drivers, and so forth who could not work from home and saw paid hours decrease under lockdown. Children in those families were also less likely to be well-equipped for online learning – prompting a scramble among volunteers to set up wi-fi hotspots, for instance, for those in need. However, the charities that customarily supplement state social services lost volunteers and donations once alert levels rose, even before the circuit-breaker (Toh 2020).

Over the course of 2020, Singapore introduced six relief packages, combining direct support for citizens with measures to prop up capital and markets. (The FY2021 budget incorporated key foci from 2020 and extended some relief measures, with initial added mitigation as Singapore backtracked on opening up midyear.) All Singaporeans received cash payments pegged to income, supplemented as appropriate by grocery vouchers and enhanced community services, with additional payments to parents of children under twenty, as well as to low-income workers and the unemployed. The government froze or relaxed various fees and use-charges, repayments and interest on government-issued student loans, and mortgage late-payment penalties for the anticipated duration of the crisis.

Much of the emphasis, though, remained on protecting jobs and businesses – a focus the pandemic warranted, but that was also in line with, and facilitated by, Singapore's customary corporatist management (e.g., of wage levels) and state and parastatal role in economic activity. Government wage-support started with the first package, then increased; by the second package, the government added support for the self-employed, complementing specific measures to help badly affected sectors such as tourism, transportation, and the arts. Training and reskilling, including targeting the self-employed, were major emphases, and the government pledged thousands of new long- and short-term public-sector jobs. By the time of parliamentary elections in July 2020, the government had tasked Singapore's National Jobs Council with launching 100,000 jobs or traineeships within a year; that promise became a cornerstone of the PAP platform. Support for businesses extended, too, to help with rental costs (e.g., for stallholders in public hawker-centers), financing (for instance, government assumption of 90 percent of the risk for loan programs for targeted sectors), and waivers or rebates of foreign-worker levies and work-permit fees. Further measures throughout the pandemic supported banks and the financial sector. Efforts stressed, too, economic resilience, including in ensuring the food supply, stockpiling health supplies, and further investment in research and development.

One might read in these stimulus packages a shift toward a social safety-net frame, with payments tied to citizenship rather than employment. However, the approach still leaned toward tax abatements over direct household transfers, notwithstanding the larger immediate stimulus (and household financial security) the latter would confer (Lim 2020). Some analyses suggested, too, that remedies did too little to support small and medium enterprises (SMEs), particularly with rent and payroll, given that SMEs represented 65 percent of the workforce and half the domestic economy (Yeoh et al. 2020). Regardless, the crisis offered a chance to consider alternatives, not least via election-campaign debates and appeals.

Yet migrant workers remained a stumbling block. The very language of pandemic management made clear the extent to which the government considered them outside the frame. Explained the minister for National Development (and co-chair of the government's COVID-19 taskforce), Singapore was "dealing with two separate infections," one "in the foreign worker dormitories" and the other "in the general population" (L. Wong 2020). Widely evident social prejudice gave this frame resonance. Public-health authorities reported these numbers separately and pegged policies, such as stages for reopening, overwhelmingly to the latter. Nor would the state even tolerate strong NGO intervention to support and provision anxious, locked-down dormitory residents, accentuating the extent to which the state assessed its pandemic-mitigation progress in terms of enfranchised-citizens' security (Han 2020a).

Rules governing foreign labor illuminate where the state-led economy yields to the market. The state treats these workers as capital, under the management of their employers; those employers, too, retain power to cancel work permits and repatriate workers, most of whom incur substantial debt to get to Singapore. Most women in the category are domestic workers, legally required to live with, and beholden to, their employers (Han 2020a). Yet the pandemic effectively socialized these costs as it revealed the obvious truth that human capital is part of the "society" that mitigation efforts address. The government did ultimately step in, for instance, thinning the population in dormitories by transferring thousands of healthy workers to now-vacant cruise ships, sports halls, and elsewhere. Those measures fell far short, however, of what Gøsta Esping-Anderson (1990, 21) terms "de-commodification of the status of individuals *vis-à-vis* the market," or ensuring individuals (for him, specifically citizens) are not mere commodities for sale in a labor market.

For its part, Malaysia saw a mix of direct outreach to citizens with strong support for capital and markets, albeit with far greater intrusion of partisan politics. However much an election-campaign motif, Singapore adopted and implemented pandemic-relief policies, as per its wont, with neither sharp dissent in parliament nor strong concerns of partisan manipulation or rent-seeking. In Malaysia, all but the initial phase of the pandemic transpired amid political turmoil, with policymaking for much of 2021 via a National Security Council, chaired by the prime minister, rather than the legislature. Moreover, overarching race-based preferential policies (for which a core objective is restructuring wealth-ownership and developing Malay capitalist and middle classes) tend to render any economic policy "political" and preclude insulated decision-making. Throughout, the sheer scope of economic damage was severe, given recurrent outbreaks and consequent shutdowns, including from a superspreader state-election campaign in September 2020. Nonessential sectors were forced to cease operations and manufacturing was capped at 60 percent capacity under MCO rules.

Pakatan Harapan announced Malaysia's first relief package just before its government collapsed; it offered help to hard-hit industries such as tourism, retail, and airlines, alongside utility discounts, income assistance, healthcare support, and other targeted spending. A series of major packages, plus supplemental measures, followed, against the backdrop of three economically paralyzing MCOs by mid-2021. Measures aimed to "benefit everyone" (NST 2020), with payments to individuals and households (targeting especially millions of low-income households and single adults, "vulnerable groups," civil servants, workers in distressed sectors such as transportation, and tertiary students), ability to withdraw pension funds without penalty, public-housing rent relief and student-loan deferrals, expanded access to unemployment benefits, flexibility in loan repayment, and tax abatements. Support for businesses included capital for SMEs, wage subsidies to sustain employment, funds for retraining and skills-development, and exemptions or deferments on taxes and contributions to human-capital development and pension funds. Also in the mix were investments in food-security infrastructure, further funding for the Ministry of Health (partly COVID-specific), and special allowances for healthcare workers and for security personnel involved in MCO-enforcement. The government pledged also to launch or sustain infrastructure projects, for multiplier effects and employment.

All told, Malaysia invested heavily in COVID-19 relief, but could not immunize economic-recovery efforts from partisan jostling. Perhaps most importantly, opponents of the then-governing coalition, and especially critics of PM Muhyiddin's suspending parliament, claimed that Malaysia would have fared better with a more secure and effective government, including being able to calibrate more finely its response were legislators able to deliberate.

Muhyiddin faulted the then-"critical stage" of the pandemic, but the fix also staved off his government's seemingly imminent collapse (Latiff and Sipalan 2021). Civil society stepped into the breach, both to support migrant workers the state neglected (Azmil and Por 2021b), as in Singapore, and with, for instance, a #kitajagakita (we look out for ourselves) campaign: diverse organizations collected and distributed donated financial and other support to the gamut of vulnerable groups (Lee 2021). For his part, rather than stress technocratic chops, and so personal support might compensate for weak confidence in his coalition, Muhyiddin embraced paternalism. He styled himself as Malaysians' *Abah* (father or daddy) and several key members of his administration with the honorific *Pak* (akin to "uncle") (Ooi 2020). Skepticism over the efficacy of Malaysia's government aside, that semantic shift encouraged citizens to relate to political leaders not as "neutral" managers, driven by and accountable for the public good, but as pseudo-familial patrons.

Indonesia's history, meanwhile, set it on a different economic-management path. Indonesia entered the pandemic with a social welfare system that was, while not expansive, much larger in scope than at any time previously. It was also a legacy of an earlier period of crisis. When the AFC hit Indonesia in 1997–98, Indonesia, with the help of the World Bank and other international actors, pulled together a system of emergency welfare and health assistance for poor citizens. Rather than dismantle this system once the crisis passed, successive national and local governments responded to social expectations in the new democratic climate and built on it incrementally, expanding, adding, and adapting health, education, cash-transfer, and other programs for proliferating categories of Indonesians. Shaping the development of this new system – birthed not as adjunct to a development state, as in Singapore, but to support citizens through their state's financial and political collapse – was also contestation between market-oriented technocrats and patronage-seeking civilian and military officials, a consistent feature of postcolonial Indonesian politics (see Murphy 2019; Rosser and Murphy 2023, 34–40; Blunt et al. 2012). Some parts of Indonesia's welfare system, reflecting the influence of technocrats, are thus relatively tightly targeted at needy Indonesians – such as cash-transfer scheme Keluarga Harapan (Family Hope) for low-income households, under the Ministry of Finance – and use mechanisms designed to reduce local officials' discretion, and thus opportunities for corruption and abuse (McCarthy and Sumarto 2018, 231–232). Other elements, such as social-assistance funds regional governments administer, are prone to capture and manipulation; local officials often distribute them in ways that achieve political goals (e.g. to reward a community's or leader's electoral support) or facilitate graft (Rosser and Wilson 2012). Indonesia's pandemic response reproduced this complexity, including the mess of competing objectives and interests that underpins it.

Whatever else it was, the emergency response was substantial. Through a series of stimulus packages, the government directed about 3.8 percent of 2020 GDP, then more in 2021, to expanded social-safety-net programs (including payments, food vouchers, and other assistance) and unemployment relief, enhanced healthcare spending, and tax relief for individuals and corporations, as well as offering access to capital, credit guarantees, loan restructuring, and tax abatements especially for SMEs and hard-hit, labor-intensive sectors such as manufacturing and tourism (IMF 2021; Olivia et al. 2020, 165–168). The central government also called upon regional governments to direct part of their own budgets to social assistance and allocated funds to villages that – building on existing patterns of community-driven development and welfare under Indonesia's Village Law – would have the flexibility to allocate funds to meet community-level needs. Most of these programs used existing welfare infrastructure and the government's centralized database on the poor, last updated in 2015 (Olivia et al. 2020, 166). In reality, targeting welfare programs to ensure that they reach (only) Indonesia's needy has historically been difficult (McCarthy and Sumarto 2018, 228–229), and was even harder in the midst of a pandemic in which millions suddenly lost livelihoods. Moreover, rather than substantially remaking or even expanding Indonesia's welfare system, as in 1997–98, the government response this time was primarily ad-hoc, pumping additional benefits largely through already-existing programs and mechanisms.

It is difficult to evaluate the extent to which these programs were subject to rent-seeking and elite capture. The breadth of distribution – with regional governments, most major ministries, and the police and military all receiving major programs to allocate – points toward a scramble by bureaucratic actors to ensure they each had access to programs (while also, of course, reflecting the depth of the crisis). Indonesia's Corruption Eradication Commission warned that the new programs themselves were vulnerable to corruption, issuing guidance on preventing and identifying malfeasance and establishing a task force to investigate possible fraud in disbursing emergency support (Rahma 2020; UNODC [2020]). Importantly, the executive order Regulation in Lieu of Law (Perppu) No. 1/2020, which the national parliament approved in May 2020, not only allowed the government to set aside a legal budget-deficit cap of 3 percent of GDP, to allow additional funding, but also exempted public officials from civil or criminal liability in relation to these duties, so long as they acted "in goodwill" (which the regulation did not define) and "according to the law" (UNODC [2020]; Ghaliya 2020). In short, COVID-19 economic relief in Indonesia saw a strong central-state role (albeit alongside some amount of delegation) and a degree of insulation from popular accountability, but not in a developmental-state vein.

More broadly, all the states considered here included in stimulus packages measures to get market capitalism back on track – loan programs and other relief for private businesses, payroll-protection funds, tax-relief, and more – yet acknowledged the limits of that model. That these relief measures also all targeted citizens, including with direct payments to compensate for stalled employment, acknowledged a key reality: state coordination and intervention were necessary not only to an effective public-health response, but also to economic sustenance and recovery. Some state efforts linked these targets, as through top-down interventions conjoining welfare support with aid for local service-providers. Thailand, for instance, heavily subsidized domestic tourism in third-quarter 2020, including specifically for healthcare workers (Chatrudee and Mongkol 2020), and Singapore issued all citizens SGD100 (USD75) vouchers to spend at local hotels and attractions.

An already established state role, such as the Singapore government's involvement in R&D, offers a ready niche for further stimulus oriented not just at keeping the population afloat, but also at recharging economic productivity. Yet such intervention is not easy to step up where the state has not commonly exercised economic leadership. Elsewhere, the private sector had to take a more active role – in the Philippines, for instance, going "beyond what the private sector is expected to do" (Suzuki 2020). There, the private sector has long been a key player in disaster response (in what is one of the world's most hazard-prone countries), beyond the government's longstanding promotion of public–private partnerships – not only given limited state resources for infrastructure projects, but also because the private sector confronts fewer bureaucratic constraints, such as public-bid requirements and audits. High levels of dependence on both labor migration (either as host or sending countries, or, as for Malaysia and Thailand, both) and tourism further complicated government responses, underlining the geographic spread of any one state's political-economic landscape. Thailand, for instance, started allowing migrant workers from neighboring states back in August 2020 and tourists (with testing and quarantine) as early as October 2020 (IMF 2021; also Termsak 2020); other states held off far longer.

Politics played a role, too. Duterte's penchant for calling out disfavored "oligarchs" (his preferred term) in his speeches seemed to spur firms to act rapidly and with a "whole-of-society" approach in order to "win over Duterte" (Reed 2020). The Ayala Group, one of the Philippines' oldest and largest conglomerates, for instance, had been embroiled in a long-standing dispute with the government about its water company, to the point that Duterte had previously threatened a military takeover. In a matter of weeks, Ayala mobilized twenty large conglomerates to join a PHP1.5 billion (USD30 million) COVID-19 response effort, including a food-distribution program, donation of medical equipment, rent-forgiveness for tenants, grace periods for telco and bank customers, and conversion of its World Trade Centre in Pasay City to a treatment facility. After Duterte apologized in early May 2020 to the tycoons he once threatened to jail, their companies' shares surged (Venzon 2020). That said, Duterte was back at it within a few weeks, in his State of the Nation address, castigating the Ayalas and another oligarch for subpar telecommunication services, and threatening to expropriate the holdings of two major telcos if their services did not quickly improve.

This renewed attack raised concerns about the uncertain future of Philippine conglomerates at an economically volatile moment. That a Duterte-aligned Congress shut down broadcast network ABS-CBN, for instance, in July 2020 – they had been off the air since their franchise expired in May – had knock-on effects, even beyond the loss of coverage: the network employed over 11,000 workers, who now faced mid-pandemic layoffs, and ABS-CBN's corporate social responsibility programs, including food and medical aid, reached more than 2 million people (Gomez 2020). In Thailand, too, PM Prayuth personally appealed to his country's "richest 20 people" to request not money, but ideas for economic-recovery programs to help Thais in need (Khaosod English 2020). Here, though, his "letter sparked ridicule for evincing a government bereft of ideas and dependent on the nation's billionaires" (ICG 2020, 22).

How to make sense of these developments? Deep crises can prompt significant change in how societies manage economic growth and distribute economic surplus: the AFC impelled welfare-system expansion in several Southeast Asian countries, not just Indonesia. The depth, breadth, and duration of the COVID-19 pandemic placed all countries under extraordinary pressure to review, repair, and in many cases, enlarge, social safety-nets, at least briefly. Nevertheless, that the *state* should come to the rescue is not a given. The Philippines presents instead a strong narrative of fiscal prudence and market solutions (Juego 2020), as Duterte lashed out at an insufficiently public-serving private sector and his critics politicized the national debt. But that approach was consonant with past patterns. Whereas the public share of health expenditure in 2019, on the eve of the pandemic, slightly exceeded 50 percent in Singapore and Malaysia and was just under half in Indonesia (and a remarkable 71.7 percent in Thailand), in the Philippines, it was 40.6 percent[30] – a key indicator of an

---

[30] See https://databank.worldbank.org/source/world-development-indicators for full time-series data.

apparently sticky inclination toward privatization of care. And most crisis-time public-sector measures were purposefully provisional, designed for short-term relief rather than long-term restructuring.

Rebuilding a pandemic-wracked economy arguably benefits from pre-existing infrastructure and precedent for a strong, minimally politicized state role. Indeed, this crisis may serve further to vindicate and legitimate state-led, technocratically oriented development. Singapore's 2020 election campaign was instructive: candidate (and economist) Jamus Lim explained that while the opposition Workers' Party platform may be but a "half-step to the left" of the PAP, that difference captured his party's preference that necessary "trade-offs" favor not capital, as per the PAP's default, but workers (Abu Baker and Chia 2020). That theme, of whose interests policies prioritize or neglect, proved especially resonant throughout the campaign, amid deep economic uncertainty – and yet both parties' platforms presumed the state to be central and largely impervious to partisan discretion. Where the state's role in economic development is less habitually strong or less able to resist rent-seeking or other elite capture, that conviction (or at least, how to implement it) remains less clear, however much desperate times summon forth novel policy approaches.

Disentangling State from Regime

Relative support for democracy has been declining globally since the 2000s, driven at least in part by frustration with its functioning and preference for an executive strong enough to supersede gridlock and polarization. This decline – which the pandemic accelerated, well beyond Southeast Asia – is germane to governance, in terms both of what leaders deliver and what citizens expect. While curfews, lockdowns, profiling, and surveillance may be appropriate interventions to stem viral contagion, such measures may expand monitoring capacity and institutionalize practices able to control citizens beyond the pandemic (see Fassin and Pandolfi 2010). The role of the police and military in enforcing lockdowns and social distancing especially in Indonesia, the Philippines, and Malaysia (where emergency rule sidestepped both parliament and precedent) was thus cause for concern. Keeping rumors and false information in check was likewise a priority for public-health authorities, yet opened the door to farther-reaching and longer-lasting curbs. Malaysia, for instance, came under fire for abusing overly sweeping anti-"fake news" enactments that lent themselves to arbitrary enforcement, turning to criminalization rather than focusing on transparency and making accurate information available.[31] Thailand, too, referred to the Computer Crime Act in its COVID-19 emergency decree: critics had previously faulted the extent to which this Act limits freedom of expression and media in the name of preventing false information (UNODC [2020]).

All that said, pandemic governance relies more on a stable, capable *state* apparatus than *regime* per se. As detailed earlier, political fumbling does seem to have worsened Malaysia's response, but even there, the issue was less whether the new administration was more or less politically liberal than its predecessor than how pulled-together it was. Recall that the director-general of health, a civil servant, kept Malaysia largely on course as partisan wrangling came to roil the political side of his ministry in early 2020.

Consider Thailand for an alternative: a military-backed post-coup government faced mass protests and skepticism as the pandemic set in, but maintained a bureaucratic core apparatus. Political leaders, rooted in the army and "especially sensitive to security, safety, and stability," took a narrowly regulatory perspective that "hid and repressed" brewing tensions and dismissed political challengers (or hamstrung them with curfews) in the name of public safety. As if channeling Duterte, the Thai prime minister adopted the rhetoric of battling an enemy, using an emergency decree that was "expected to be implemented in wartime situations" and emphasizing behaving well for the good of the country. As in the Philippines, too, he blamed the poor, who really had no choice but to keep working, for spreading infection (Piyapong and Pobsook 2020). But the Centre for COVID-19 Situation Administration the prime minister headed incorporated input from medical doctors, under successive emergency decrees (ICG 2020, 19). The result was a fairly effective epidemiological and economic response, however much the government used "scientific evidence" not only to support its containment efforts, "but also to legitimise political messages and the moral guidance that was being offered to the population" (Piyapong and Pobsook 2020). Its pandemic response allowed the military-backed government to consolidate control and project "an image of confidence" even as it quashed protests, suggesting (further) democratic regression as not antithetical to crisis management. All the same, the effort left the government more vulnerable to losing political legitimacy, with potentially "painful and far-reaching consequences" (ICG 2020, 21) – further complicating any assessment of the extent to which an illiberal turn matters.

In short, disarticulating state from regime clarifies the lack of clear connection between quality of democracy and quality of pandemic governance,

---

[31] E.g., https://www.article19.org/resources/malaysia-stop-using-repressive-laws-to-counter-misinformation-about-coronavirus/.

a finding that might temper concerns about the policy implications of democratic decline. On the one hand, a well-functioning bureaucracy can compensate for less-competent political leadership, and both democratic and illiberal modes of decision-making have their advantages. New or established democracies might not follow unpopular science-backed policy prescriptions or avoid pitfalls such as corruption; other factors, from relative national income to technological level, may matter even more than regime, including how well-developed and durable "public institutions of trust, transparency, accountability and government effectiveness" are (Burnell 2012, 827, 829). On the other hand, the crisis's scale and complexity called for both technocratic rectitude and sensitivity to popular doubts and needs, which a premise of "apolitical" technocratic management could accommodate only poorly. The former, technocracy, lends cover to democratic backsliding; the latter may have spurred pushback in favor of liberalizing reforms as the region edged toward recovery.

Implications for Crisis-management

States' responses to COVID-19 not only offer insight into in-the-moment governance and behavioral patterns but will also help to shape subsequent praxis, given inevitable crises to come. In particular, an approach to development that centers the state and "prioritse[s] the economic over the political" seems likely to hold continuing sway as states confront new challenges (Beeson 2010, 281). Habits of governance do not disappear without a trace; past praxis helps to explain why states governed the pandemic especially adeptly or poorly, as well as what lies ahead, in a world of next-generation public-health, ecological, and other calamities.

Recent experience suggests two primary implications. First, politics tempers priorities and processes, but how states respond under pressure still demonstrates a high degree of institutional path-dependency. One might expect the response to later crises, as with this one, to resonate with an enduring repertoire, among both leaders (e.g., recourse to securitization in those states with a history of military engagement in politics) and citizens. One might argue that the limited propensity toward a strong regional or otherwise transnational response to what is clearly a boundary-blind emergency likewise reflects habit first and foremost. In this case, the salience of trans-border populations made including noncitizens in a public-health response essential. Moreover, the reality is that no one country could recover economically on its own; the extent of intra-regional labor migration, higher-education markets, supply chains, trade flows, and tourism mandated at least some extent of (Southeast) Asian coordination (Menon 2020). Yet although regional and global organizations, from ASEAN to the WHO, played roles, states focused overwhelmingly on managing matters within their own borders. Even technocratic Singapore failed to shift registers sufficiently to embrace this broader frame. In fact, this period was an especially rocky one for global collaboration, particularly given Trump-administration isolationism and US–China rivalry, notwithstanding regional and "minilateral" cross-regional coordination, including the signing of the Regional Comprehensive Economic Partnership (RCEP) agreement in November 2020 (Tiberghien 2021, 22–29, 67–70).

Second, but relatedly: regardless of distinct starting points, the trend appears to be toward illiberalism overall. It may be difficult to disentangle technocracy from authoritarianism where a technocratic legacy is top-down, opaque governance and reliance on performance legitimacy. Yet one may find in the extent to which central-government leaders seek to personalize agency rather than rely on parliamentary or other institutional decision-making, or to which they invite and empower or discourage decentralized innovation, evidence of embrace or rejection of illiberalism – quite apart from whether scientific expertise, the public good, or personal interest guides policymaking. Pandemic governance across Southeast Asia indicated overall a propensity toward consolidating authority, regardless of how one might characterize the policies that emerged. That same impetus seems likely to resurface with future crises, given the recourse to learned behaviors and pathways that the need for quick, decisive action impels. In this case, a strong, top-down response to SARS worked well; experience of COVID-19 reinforced that precedent, representing a new waystation on a familiar path.

Conclusions

Navigating "hard times" shines a spotlight on structures and habits that define how states respond to emergencies, as well as opportunities for governance innovations. Evidence suggests that the COVID-19 pandemic amplified rather than transformed the character of states and their policymaking apparatus: institutional and normative path-dependency channel states' efforts in a crisis, without forestalling the possibility also of adaptation. This conclusion emerges partly by process of elimination. State capacity and resources – already commonly stretched as concepts – are insufficient explanations, nor is it clear which indicators for these would be most germane and comparable (Cingolani 2018). Systemic variables such as regime type – how liberal or not a government is, or, for instance (implicit in the discussion above, but not a focus), whether presidential or parliamentary in structure (Eaton 2000) – offer insufficient analytical leverage, at least beyond the general conclusion that leaders carry more weight in weakly institutionalized systems. That inadequacy reflects both normal variability in form and function and the fact that other institutional features may vary differently and might matter more. One needs to look elsewhere to account for relative agility, responsiveness, coordination, and durability in policy responses. Southeast Asian experience suggests four summary claims.

First, the background context against which the pandemic unfolded shaped states' immediate response. In particular, policymakers' *bases of legitimacy* and *governing approach* informed COVID-19 politics. Malaysia and Singapore have historically relied on performance legitimacy, albeit heavily tempered in Malaysia by identitarian considerations. Both took fairly quick, decisive action on widespread, state-funded testing, extensive contact-tracing, and strict, enforced travel bans and lockdowns. Given both strong bureaucratic infrastructure and, in Malaysia, a shaky political transition that rendered personalized grandstanding less possible, institutional forces, both elected and otherwise, governed these states' responses. And yet in Singapore, bureaucratic authority proved less buffeted by politics than in Malaysia; Singapore's full-fledged developmental-state heritage kicked into action. In contrast, Indonesia's and the Philippines' populist-inclined leaders' priorities held sway. Jokowi's overriding objective was safeguarding the economy; Duterte's was further concentration of power in the executive. That the military has played central roles in government in both these postauthoritarian countries, too – unlike in Singapore or Malaysia – facilitated or even encouraged a public-security orientation, while also buffering the leader at the top.

Second, the *fact of resources matters less than how they are deployed*. Most obviously, a high GDP, but with limited investment in healthcare or related services, may matter little when test-kits, personal protective equipment, vaccines, or healthcare workers are in short supply on the global market. Homing in more narrowly, too: *distribution* of relevant resources is key; a virus does not discriminate. Singapore's experience exemplifies (though hardly uniquely) the consequences of ignoring public-health concerns among highly vulnerable non-citizens. Meanwhile, less-wealthy Vietnam's cost-effective strategy of empowering a national steering committee, ensuring clear communications, closing borders, and quickly ramping up temperature-screening and testing (with low-cost, locally made test-kits), while enforcing stringent contact-tracing and quarantine, targeted lockdowns, mask-wearing, and social-distancing, proved resources potentially secondary to decisive action (Klingler-Vidra and Tran 2020; Quach and Hoang 2020).

Third, these cases point to the *(missed) opportunity of empowering subnational authorities*, including to encourage community-level innovations. While decentralization has been a key pillar in public-sector reform in both

Indonesia and the Philippines for decades now, COVID-19 exposed how central governments may hinder subnational political actors from taking decisive action, constraining the benefits devolution aims to deliver. Meanwhile, Malaysia's substantially centralized federation came under strain when states pushed back against central-government policies insufficiently in line with local realities. All three cases demonstrate the shortcomings of overreliance on the center in determining policies, especially absent a strong effort to build broad consensus – a potential frailty of the generally centralized developmental-state model. What took place was less coordination across tiers than vertical imposition, manifest in (real or threatened) punishment of local governments that failed to comply with national directives. Such a framework constrains rather than enabling adaptation and innovation. In contrast, Thailand granted provincial governors "significant authority" over imposition of lockdowns, effectively complementing top-down coordination with more targeted interventions – and perhaps also furthering ruling-party efforts to cultivate provincial voters' support (Hatchakorn and Viengrat 2021; ICG 2020, 19).

Fourth and finally, *building consensus* on *why* everyone should do their part, and what that part entails, is key, both in a public-health emergency and in looming challenges such as mitigating climate change. The only incremental accretion of accurate information about the virus made that effort all the more challenging. However, clear messaging and transparency to make obvious the link between actions and outcomes build trust, facilitating compliance, and allow more effective epidemiological or other interventions. Singapore modeled that approach in its accessible, straightforward, regularly updated information, capitalizing on general habituation to, and faith in, government intervention.

Pundits have been quick to foretell the transformative potential of the COVID 19 pandemic. A global health emergency prompted a rethink of economic systems, political structures, and national priorities. The very real impact that this crisis, and the soul-searching it set in motion, has had and will continue to have, among states, communities, and individuals, is indubitable. However, as the cases presented here demonstrate, institutional path-dependence goes far to explain differences in governance – both modes adopted and how effective they have been. Put to the test, these governments remain more likely to belt out theme songs than swiftly change their tunes. Given that reality, a plausible explanation for the relative performance of specific Southeast Asian states rests not in culture, the fact of experience of SARS, or authoritarian predilections per se but in the decision-making legacies, priorities, and functional capacities of developmental statehood; the distribution of relevant authority; and the sort of framing and approach the character of state–society relations favored. However necessarily multifaceted that diagnosis, it at least suggests that high-performance growth trajectories of the past, or adopting cognate institutional strategies now, may reap payoffs still.

References

Abu Baker, Jalelah and Lianne Chia. 2020. "GE2020: PAP, PSP, WP and SDP Candidates Take Part in 'Live' General Election Debate. *CNA*, July 2, https://www.channelnewsasia.com/singapore/ge2020-live-broadcast-political-debate-pap-wp-sdp-psp-942441.

Abuza, Zachary, and Bridget Welsh. 2020. "The Politics of Pandemic in Southeast Asia." *The Diplomat*, June 2, https://thediplomat.com/2020/06/the-politics-of-pandemic-in-southeast-asia/.

Adjie, Moch. Fiqih Prawira, Arya Dipa, and Ardilla Syakriah. 2020. "Jakarta, West Java Governors Doubt Central Govt COVID-19 Figures." *The Jakarta Post*, April 5, https://www.thejakartapost.cm/news/2020/04/04/jakarta-west-java-governors-doubt-central-govt-covid-19-figures.html.

Agence France-Presse. 2020. "'It's Insulting': Indonesia Criticizes US Study Concerns Over No Coronavirus Cases." *Jakarta Post*, 12 July, https://www.thejakartapost.com/news/2020/02/12/its-insulting-indonesia-criticizes-us-study-concerns-over-no-coronavirus-cases.html.

Ainaa Aiman. 2020. "51% Spike in MCO Arrests, Says Ismail Sabri." *Free Malaysia Today*, June 4, https://www.freemalaysiatoday.com/category/nation/2020/04/06/51-spike-in-mco-arrests-says-ismail-sabri/.

Al Jazeera. 2020. "Malaysia to Expel Bangladeshi Who Featured in Al Jazeera Report." *Al Jazeera*, July 25, https://www.aljazeera.com/news/2020/7/25/malaysia-to-expel-bangladeshi-who-featured-in-al-jazeera-report.

——— 2021. "'It Will Get Very Bad': Experts Warn on Indonesia COVID Surge." *Al Jazeera*, June 18, https://www.aljazeera.com/news/2021/6/18/indonesia-covid.

Amporn Marddent and Vithaya Arporn. "'Or Sor Mor' and 'Ai Khai': Frontliners in Thailand's Fight against COVID-19." *Contemporary Southeast Asia* 43(1): 24–30.

Amsden, Alice. 1991. "Diffusion of Development: The Late-Industrializing Model and Greater East Asia." *American Economic Review* 81(2): 282–286.

Anand, Ram. 2021. "Malaysia's Raids on Undocumented Migrants Raise Vaccination Fears." *Straits Times*, June 13, https://www.straitstimes.com/asia/se-asia/malaysias-raids-on-undocumented-migrants-raise-vaccination-fears.

Ananthalakshmi, A. and Rozanna Latiff. 2020. "Rohingya Targeted in Malaysia as Coronavirus Stokes Xenophobia." Reuters, May 22, https://www.reu

ters.com/article/us-health-coronavirus-malaysia-rohingya/rohingya-targeted-in-malaysia-as-coronavirus-stokes-xenophobia-idUSKBN22Z00K.

Aspinall, Edward. 2014. "Health Care and Democratization in Indonesia." *Democratization*. 21(5): 803–823.

Aspinall, Edward, Nicole Curato, Diego Fossati, Eve Warburton, and Meredith Weiss. 2021. "COVID-19 in Southeast Asia: Public Health, Social Impacts, and Political Attitudes." Policy briefing – SEARBO. Canberra: New Mandala.

Aspinwall, Nick. 2020. "Police Abuse, Prison Deaths Draw Concern as Philippines Tightens Lockdown Measures." *The Diplomat*, https://thediplomat.com/2020/04/police-abuse-prison-deaths-draw-concern-as-philippines-tightens-lockdown-measures/.

Aubrecht, Paul, Jan Essink, Mitja Kovac, and Ann-Sophie Vandenberghe. 2020. "Centralized and Decentralized Responses to COVID-19 in Federal Systems: US and EU Comparisons." Law & Economics of Covid-19 Working Paper series, 04/2020, https://papers.ssrn.com/sol3/papers.cfm?abstract_id=3584182&gt.

Azmil Tayeb and Por Heong Hong. 2021a. "Malaysia: Improvised Pandemic Policies and Democratic Regression." In *Covid-19 in Asia: Law and Policy Challenges*, edited by Victor V. Ramraj, 321–34. Oxford: Oxford University Press.

2021b. "Xenophobia and COVID-19 Aid to Refugee and Migrant Communities in Penang." *Contemporary Southeast Asia* 43(1): 77–82.

Bäck, Hanna and Axel Hadenius. 2008. "Democracy and State Capacity: Exploring a J-Shaped Relationship." *Governance* 21(1): 1–24.

Baker, Jacqui. 2023. "Reformasi Reversal: Structural Drivers of Democratic Decline in Jokowi's Middle-Income Indonesia." *Bulletin of Indonesian Economic Studies* 59(3): 341–364.

Barr, Michael D. 2000. "Lee Kuan Yew and the 'Asian Values' Debate." *Asian Studies Review* 24(3): 309–334.

2008. "Singapore: The Limits of a Technocratic Approach to Health Care." *Journal of Contemporary Asia* 38(3): 395–416.

BBC. 2021. "Malaysia Deports Myanmar Nationals Despite Court Order." *BBC*, February 24, www.bbc.com/news/world-asia-56178270.

Beech, Hannah. 2020. "No One Knows What Thailand Is Doing Right, but So Far, It's Working." *New York Times*, July 16, https://www.nytimes.com/2020/07/16/world/asia/coronavirus-thailand-photos.html.

Beeson, Mark. 2010. "The Coming of Environmental Authoritarianism." *Environmental Politics* 19(2): 276–294.

Berengaut, Ariana A. 2020. "Democracies Are Better at Fighting Outbreaks." *The Atlantic*, February 24, https://www.theatlantic.com/ideas/archive/2020/02/why-democracies-are-better-fighting-outbreaks/606976/.

Bernama. 2020. "Malaysia to Deport Illegal Immigrants Tested Negative for COVID-19 – Ismail Sabri." *Bernama*, May 26, https://www.bernama.com/en/news.php?id=1845008.

Bersih. 2020a. "Covid-19 Gifts Raise Questions of Accountability and Power Abuse." Press statement, April 1, https://www.bersih.org/bersih-2-0-press-statement-1-april-2020-covid-19-gifts-raise-questions-of-accountability-and-power-abuse/ (accessed July 18, 2020).

——— 2020b. "Police Need to Be More Restrained toward Volunteers." Press Statement, April 30, https://www.bersih.org/press-release-from-bersih-2-0-30-april-2020-police-need-to-be-more-restrained-towards-volunteers/ (accessed July 18, 2020).

Bisnis.com. 2020. "DPR setujui tambahan anggaran Rp3,2 triliun untuk tni tangani COVID-19." *Bisnis.com*, April 15, https://kabar24.bisnis.com/read/20200415/15/1227554/dpr-setujui-tambahan-anggaran-rp32-triliun-untuk-tni-tangani-covid-19.

Bland, Ben. 2020. "Jokowi Needs to Change Strategy." *Straits Times*, July 18, https://www.straitstimes.com/opinion/jokowi-needs-to-change-strategy.

Blunt, Peter, Mark Turner, and Henrik Lindroth. 2012. "Patronage's Progress in Post-Soeharto Indonesia." *Public Administration and Development* 32: 64–81.

Boin, Arjen, Paul 't Hart, Eric Stern, and Bengt Sundelius. 2016. *The Politics of Crisis Management: Public Leadership under Pressure*. Cambridge: Cambridge University Press.

Boudreau, Vincent. 1996. "Northern Theory, Southern Protest: Opportunity Structure Analysis in Cross-National Perspective." *Mobilization* 1(2): 175–189.

Briantika, Adi. 2020. "Kapolri Terbitkan Aturan Penghinaan Jokowi & Pejabat Saat Corona." Kumparan, April 5, https://tirto.id/kapolri-terbitkan-aturan-penghinaan-jokowi-pejabat-saat-corona-eK7a.

Burnell, Peter. 2012. "Democracy, Democratization and Climate Change: Complex Relationships." *Democratization* 19(5): 813–842.

Cabato, Regine. 2021. "Philippines' Duterte Threatens to Arrest Anyone Refusing to Get Vaccinated." *Washington Post*, June 22, https://www.washingtonpost.com/world/asia_pacific/duterte-philippines-arrest-vaccine/2021/06/22/9ac3eed8-d337-11eb-b39f-05a2d776b1f4_story.html.

Camoens, Austin. 2020. "Ismail Sabri: 38 Nabbed for Flouting Recovery MCO in June 29." *The Star*, June 30, https://thestar.com.my/news/nation/2020/06/30/ismail-sabri-39-nabbed-for-flouting-recovery-mco-on-june-29.

Cejas, Gabriel. 2020. "Ormoc Mayor Richard Gomez Slams Government's Balik Probinsya Program." *Rappler*, May 25, https://www.rappler.com/philippines/261929-ormoc-mayor-richard-gomez-slams-balik-probinsya-program/.

Chan, Hin-yeung. 2013. "Crisis Politics in Authoritarian Regimes: How Crises Catalyse Changes under the State–Society Interactive Framework." *Journal of Contingencies and Crisis Management* 21(4): 200–210.

Chatrudee Theparat and Mongkol Bangprapa. 2020. "Domestic Tourism Gets Triple Booster." *Bangkok Post*, June 17, https://www.bangkokpost.com/thailand/general/1935988/domestic-tourism-gets-triple-booster.

Chua Beng Huat. 1995. *Communitarian Ideology and Democracy in Singapore*. New York: Routledge.

——— 2017. *Liberalism Disavowed: Communitarianism and State Capitalism in Singapore*. Ithaca: Cornell University Press.

Cingolani, Luciana. 2018. "The Role of State Capacity in Development Studies." *Journal of Development Perspectives* 2(1–2): 88–114.

Cochrane, Joe. 2020. "'We owe it to God': as Indonesia Prays, How Is It Keeping the Coronavirus at Bay?" *South China Morning Post*, February 18, https://www.scmp.com/week-asia/health-environment/article/3051068/we-owe-it-god-indonesia-prays-how-it-keeping.

Coronel, Sheila, Mariel Padilla, David Mora, and Stabile Institute for Journalism. 2019. "The Uncounted Dead of Duterte's Drug War." *The Atlantic*. August 19, https://www.theatlantic.com/international/archive/2019/08/philippines-dead-rodrigo-duterte-drug-war/595978/.

Crispin, Shawn W. 2020. "Malaysian Journalist Faces Six Years in Prison over COVID-19 Facebook Posts." Committee to Protect Journalists, May 5, https://cpj.org/2020/05/malaysian-journalist-faces-six-years-in-prison-ove/.

Dancel, Raul. 2020. "Coronavirus: Duterte Threatens Martial Law-Like Lockdown in Philippines as Many Flout Controls." *Straits Times*, April 17, https://www.straitstimes.com/asia/se-asia/coronavirus-duterte-threatens-martial-law-like-lockdown-in-philippines-as-many-flout.

Daniel, Thomas. 2020. "COVID-19 Highlights the Plight of Malaysia's Refugees." *East Asia Forum*, May 18, https://www.eastasiaforum.org/2020/05/18/covid-19-highlights-the-plight-of-malaysias-refugees.

Davies, Sarah E. 2019. *Containing Contagion: The Politics of Disease Outbreaks in Southeast Asia*. Baltimore: Johns Hopkins University Press.

Dayrit, Manuel M., Liezel P. Lagrada, Oscar F. Picazo, Melahi C. Pons, and Mario C. Villaverde. 2018. *The Philippines Health System Review*. New Delhi: World Health Organization, Regional Office for South-East Asia.

Dayrit, Manuel M., Ronald U. Mendoza, and Sheena A. Valenzuela. 2020. "The Importance of Effective Risk Communication and Transparency: Lessons from the Dengue Vaccine Controversy in the Philippines." *Journal of Public Health Policy* 41(3): 252–267.

Deloitte Indonesia. 2019. "Ensuring the Sustainability of JKN-KIS for the Indonesian People." *Deloitte Indonesia Perspectives*, September, https://www2.deloitte.com/content/dam/Deloitte/id/Documents/about-deloitte/id-about-dip-edition-1-chapter-1-en-sep2019.pdf.

Deyo, Frederic C. 1989. *Beneath the Miracle: Labor Subordination in the New Asian Industrialism*. Berkeley: University of California Press.

Ding, Emily. 2020. "Undocumented Migrants and Refugees Are Caught in the Crossfire of Malaysia's Coronavirus Response and a Xenophobic Backlash." *Foreign Policy*, June 19, https://foreignpolicy.com/2020/06/19/malaysias-coronavirus-scapegoats/.

Diokno-Sicat, Justine, and Ricxie B. Maddawin. 2018. "A Survey of Literature on Philippine Decentralization." PIDS Discussion Paper Series, no. 2018–23 (December). Quezon City: Philippines Institute for Development Studies.

Djalante, Riyante, et al. 2020. "COVID-19 and ASEAN Responses: Comparative Policy Analysis." *Progress in Disaster Science* 8, https://doi.org/10.1016/j.pdisas.2020.100129.

Doner, Richard F., Bryan K. Ritchie, and Dan Slater. 2005. "Systemic Vulnerability and the Origins of Developmental States: Northeast and Southeast Asia in Comparative Perspective." *International Organization* 59: 327–361.

Eaton, Kent. 2000. "Review: Parliamentarism versus Presidentialism in the Policy Arena." *Comparative Politics* 32(3): 355–376.

———. 2001. "Political Obstacles to Decentralization: Evidence from Argentina and the Philippines." *Development and Change* 32(1): 101–127

Economist. 2012. "Rethinking the Welfare State: Asia's Next Revolution." *The Economist*, September 8, https://www.economist.com/leaders/2012/09/08/asias-next-revolution.

———. 2021. "Tracking Covid-19 Excess Deaths across Countries." *The Economist*, May 11, https://www.economist.com/graphic-detail/coronavirus-excess-deaths-tracker.

Esping-Anderson, Gøsta. 1990. *Three Worlds of Welfare Capitalism*. Princeton: Princeton University Press.

Evans, Peter B. 2014. "The Capability Enhancing Developmental State: Concepts and National Trajectories." In *The South Korean Development Experience: Beyond Aid*, edited by Eun Mee Kim and Pil Ho Kim, 83–110. London: Palgrave Macmillan.

Evans, Peter, and Patrick Heller. 2019. "The State and Development." In *Asian Transformations: An Inquiry Into the Development of Nations*, edited by Deepak Nayyar, 109–135. Oxford: Oxford University Press.

Farisa, Fitria Chusna 2020. "Kemendagri Minta Pemda Realokasi Anggaran Penanganan Covid-19 dalam 7 Hari ke Depan." *Kompas*, April 3, https://nasional.kompas.com/read/2020/04/03/19325071/kemendagri-minta-pemda-realokasi-anggaran-penanganan-covid-19-dalam-7-hari.

Fassin, Didier, and Pandolfi, Mariella. 2010. *Contemporary States of Emergency: The Politics of Military And Humanitarian Interventions*. New York: Zone Books.

Fenner, Sofia. 2020. "State, Regime, Government, and Society in COVID-19 Response: Establishing Baseline Expectations." *Duck of Minerva*, March 17, https://duckofminerva.com/2020/03/state-regime-government-and-society-in-covid-19-response-establishing-baseline-expectations.html.

Fidler, David P. 2010. "Negotiating Equitable Access to Influenza Vaccines: Global Health Diplomacy and the Controversies Surrounding Avian Influenza H5n1 and Pandemic Influenza H1n1." *PLoS Medicine* 7(5): e1000247.

Fisher, Dale. 2020. "Why Singapore's Coronavirus Response Worked – and What We Can All Learn." *The Conversation*, March 18, https://theconversation.com/why-singapores-coronavirus-response-worked-and-what-we-can-all-learn-134024.

Fukuyama, Francis. 2020. "The Pandemic and Political Order: It Takes a State." *Foreign Affairs*, July/August, https://www.foreignaffairs.com/articles/world/2020-06-09/pandemic-and-political-order.

Geddie, John, and Aradhana Aravindan. 2020. "In Singapore, Migrant Coronavirus Cases Highlight Containment Weak Link." Reuters, April 15, https://www.reuters.com/article/us-health-coronavirus-singapore-migrants/in-singapore-migrant-coronavirus-cases-highlight-containment-weak-link-idUSKCN21X19G.

Ghaliya, Ghina. 2020. "House Grills Govt over 'Unconstitutional' Perppu." *Jakarta Post*, April 30, https://www.thejakartapost.com/news/2020/04/30/house-grills-govt-over-unconstitutional-perppu.html.

Gomez, Jim. 2020. "Lawmakers Vote to Close Down Philippines' Largest TV Network." *The Diplomat*, July 10, https://thediplomat.com/2020/07/lawmakers-vote-to-close-down-philippines-largest-tv-network/.

Gopinath, Gita. 2020. "The Great Lockdown: Worst Economic Downturn since the Great Depression." *IMF Blog*, April 14, https://blogs.imf.org/2020/04/14/the-great-lockdown-worst-economic-downturn-since-the-great-depression/.

Gotinga, J. C. 2020. "Vico Sotto on NBI Summons: We Complied with All Directives." *Rappler*, April 1, https://www.rappler.com/philippines/256680-vico-sotto-response-nbi-summons-april-1-2020/.

Gourevitch, Peter. 1986. *Politics in Hard Times: Comparative Responses to International Economic Crises*. Ithaca, NY: Cornell University Press.

Graham, Colum. 2020. "Indonesia's Agro Nationalism in the Pandemic." *New Mandala*, June 4, https://www.newmandala.org/indonesias-agro-nationalism-in-the-pandemic/.

Greer, Scott L., Elizabeth J. King, and Elize Massard da Fonseca. 2021. "Introduction: Explaining Pandemic Response." In *Coronavirus Politics: The Comparative Politics and Policy of COVID-19*, edited by Scott L. Greer, Elizabeth J. King, Elize Massard da Fonseca, and Andre Peralta-Santos, 3–33. Ann Arbor: University of Michigan Press.

Greer, Scott L., Elizabeth J. King, Elize Massard da Fonseca, and Andre Peralta-Santos. 2020. "The Comparative Politics of COVID-19: The Need to Understand Government Responses." *Global Public Health*, 15 (9), 1413–1416, https://doi.org/10.1080/17441692.2020.1783340.

Gudmalin, Cadmilo, Lizan Perante-Calina, Joven Balbosa, Joel Mangahas, and Maria Aloha Samoza. 2021. "Protecting the Poor and Vulnerable against the Pandemic." ADBI Development Case Study No. 2021–3. Tokyo: Asian Development Bank.

Hadiz, Vedi R. 2010. *Localising Power in Post-Authoritarian Indonesia: A Southeast Asia Perspective*. Stanford, CA: Stanford University Press.

Haggard, Stephan. 2018. *Developmental States*. New York: Cambridge University Press.

——— 2015. "The Developmental State is Dead: Long Live the Developmental State." In *Advances in Comparative Historical Analysis*, edited by James Mahoney and Kathleen Thelen, 39–66. Cambridge: Cambridge University Press.

Haines, Monamie Bhadra, and Hallam Stevens. 2020. "Does Singapore Need Mandatory Contact Tracing Apps?" *New Mandala*, May 18, https://www.newmandala.org/does-singapore-need-mandatory-contact-tracing-apps/.

Hakim, Rakhmat Nur. 2020. "Luhut: Dari Hasil Modelling, Virus Corona Tak Kuat Hidup di Cuaca Indonesia." *Kompas*, April 2, https://nasional.kompas.com/read/2020/04/02/15275601/luhut-dari-hasil-modelling-virus-corona-tak-kuat-hidup-di-cuaca-indonesia.

Halim, Devina. 2020. "Polri Klaim Telah 205.502 Kali Bubarkan Massa Selama Wabah Covid-19." *Kompas*, April 14, https://nasional.kompas.com/read/2020/04/13/20275441/polri-klaim-telah-205502-kali-bubarkan-massa-selama-wabah-covid-19.

Hall, Rosalie Arcala. 2022. "Camouflage in the Streets: Emergency Powers, the Military, and the Philippines' COVID-19 Pandemic Response." *Philippine Political Science Journal* 43(2): 168–191.

Han, Kirsten. 2020a. "A Perfect Storm for an Outbreak." *We, the Citizens*, April 23, https://wethecitizens.substack.com/p/wtc-long-read-a-perfect-storm-for.

2020b. "Singapore Is Trying to Forget Migrant Workers Are People." *Foreign Policy*, May 6, https://foreignpolicy.com/2020/05/06/singapore-coronavirus-pandemic-migrant-workers/.

Hapal, Karl. 2021. "The Philippines' COVID-19 Response: Securitising the Pandemic and Disciplining the Pasaway." *Journal of Current Southeast Asian Affairs* 40(2): 224–244.

Harris, Joseph. 2015. "'Developmental Capture' of the State: Explaining Thailand's Universal Coverage Policy." *Journal of Health Politics, Policy and Law* 40(1): 165–193.

2017. *Achieving Access: Professional Movements and the Politics of Health Universalism*. Ithaca, NY: Cornell University Press.

Hasani, Asip. 2020. "Greater Surabaya PSBB Rendered Useless as East Java Allows Mass Prayers: Epidemiologists." *Jakarta Post*, May 18, https://www.thejakartapost.com/news/2020/05/18/greater-surabaya-psbb-rendered-useless-as-east-java-allows-mass-prayers-epidemiologists.html.

Hatchakorn Vongsayan and Viengrat Nethipo. 2021. "The Roles of Thailand's City Municipalities in the COVID-19 Crisis." *Contemporary Southeast Asia* 43(1): 15–23.

Hayllar, Mark Richard. 2007. "Governance and Community Engagement in Managing SARS in Hong Kong." *Asian Journal of Political Science* 15(1): 39–67.

Hill, Hal, ed. 2015. *Regional Dynamics in a Decentralized Indonesia*. Singapore: Institute of Southeast Asian Studies.

Ho, Hang Kei. 2020. "COVID-19 Pandemic Management Strategies and Outcomes in East Asia and the Western World: The Scientific State,

Democratic Ideology, and Social Behavior." *Frontiers in Sociology* 5: 575588.

Holliday, Ian. 2000. "Productivist Welfare Capitalism: Social Policy in East Asia." *Political Studies* 48(4): 706–723.

Holmes, Roland D., and Paul D. Hutchcroft. 2020. "A Failure of Execution." *Inside Story*, April 4, https://insidestory.org.au/a-failure-of-execution/.

Huang, Yasheng, Meicen Sun, and Yuze Sui. 2020. "How Digital Contact Tracing Slowed Covid-19 in East Asia." *Harvard Business Review*, April 15, https://hbr.org/2020/04/how-digital-contact-tracing-slowed-covid-19-in-east-asia.

Human Rights Watch. 2020. "Cambodia: Covid-19 Spurs Bogus 'Fake News' Arrests." April 29, https://www.hrw.org/news/2020/04/29/cambodia-covid-19-spurs-bogus-fake-news-arrests.

ICG. 2020. "COVID-19 and a Possible Political Reckoning in Thailand." Asia Report No. 309. Brussels: International Crisis Group.

IMF. 2021. "Policy Responses to COVID-19." International Monetary Fund, https://www.imf.org/en/Topics/imf-and-covid19/Policy-Responses-to-COVID-19 (last updated July 2, 2021; accessed September 22, 2025).

IPAC. 2020. "COVID-19 and Conflict in Papua." IPAC Short Briefing No. 2. Institute for Policy Analysis of Conflict, April 13, https://tile.loc.gov/storage-services/service/gdc/gdcovop/2021307198/2021307198.pdf.

Jaffrey, Sana. 2019. "Leveraging the Leviathan: Politics of Impunity and the Rise of Vigilantism in Democratic Indonesia." PhD dissertation. University of Chicago.

———. 2020. "Coronavirus Blunders in Indonesia Turn Crisis into Catastrophe." Carnegie Endowment, April 20, https://carnegieendowment.org/2020/04/29/coronavirus-blunders-in-indonesia-turn-crisis-into-catastrophe-pub-81684.

Jakarta Globe. 2022. "Flashback to New Order: Active Military Officers Can Become Regional Leaders." *Jakarta Globe*, May 26, https://jakartaglobe.id/news/flashback-to-new-order-active-military-officers-can-become-regional-leaders.

Jakarta Post. 2020. "COVID-19: Surabaya Mayor Feuds with East Java Governor over Mobile PCR Labs." *Jakarta Post*, May 31, https://www.thejakartapost.com/news/2020/05/31/covid-19-surabaya-mayor-feuds-with-east-java-governor-over-mobile-pcr-labs.html.

Johns Hopkins Center for Health Security. 2019. *Global Health Security Index 2019: Building Collective Action and Accountability*, https://www.ghsindex.org/wp-content/uploads/2019/10/2019-Global-Health-Security-Index.pdf.

References

Johnson, Chalmers. 1982. *MITI and the Japanese Miracle: The Growth of Industrial Policy, 1925–1975*. Stanford, CA: Stanford University Press.

Juego, Bonn. 2020. "Addressing the Pandemic in the Philippines Necessitates a New Economic Paradigm." *Developing Economies*, June 13, https://developingeconomics.org/2020/06/13/addressing-the-pandemic-in-the-philippines-necessitates-a-new-economic-paradigm/.

Khaosod English. 2020. "Leaked Letter: Prayut Asks Top Tycoons for Virus Rescue Plans." *Khaosod English*, April 21, https://www.khaosodenglish.com/politics/2020/04/21/leaked-letter-prayut-asks-top-tycoons-for-virus-rescue-plans/.

Klingler-Vidra, Robyn and Ba-Linh Tran. 2020. "Vietnam Has Reported No Coronavirus Deaths – How?" *The Conversation*, April 21, https://theconversation.com/vietnam-has-reported-no-coronavirus-deaths-how-136646.

Kristiansen, Stein, and Purwo Santoso. 2006. "Surviving Decentralisation? Impacts of Regional Autonomy on Health Service Provision in Indonesia." *Health Policy* 77: 247–259.

Kumparan. 2020. "Daftar 7 Wilayah yang Pengajuan PSBB-nya Ditolak Terawan." *Kumparan News*, April 20, https://kumparan.com/kumparannews/daftar-7-wilayah-yang-pengajuan-psbb-nya-ditolak-terawan-1tG78hjwvrv/full.

Kwon, Huck-ju. 2007. "Transforming the Developmental Welfare State in East Asia." DESA Working Paper No. 40. New York: United Nations Department of Economic & Social Affairs.

Laksmana, Evan, and Rage Taufika. 2020. "How 'Militarized' Is Indonesia's COVID-19 Management?" *Jakarta Post*, May 27, https://www.thejakartapost.com/academia/2020/05/27/how-militarized-is-indonesias-covid-19-management.html.

Latiff, Rozanna, and Joseph Sipalan. 2021. "Malaysia Declares Emergency to Curb Virus, Shoring Up Government." Reuters, January 11, https://www.reuters.com/article/us-health-coronavirus-malaysia-idUSKBN29H06G.

Lazar, Nomi Claire. 2020. "Singapore Excels at Transparency While Confronting Spread of COVID-19." *Toronto Star*, March 4, https://www.thestar.com/opinion/contributors/2020/03/04/singapore-excels-at-transparency-while-confronting-spread-of-covid-19.html.

Lee, Clarissa Ai Ling. 2021. "Malaysia's #Kitajagakita Invigorates Political Activism and Tackles Apathy." *Fulcrum*, September 14, https://fulcrum.sg/malaysias-kitajagakita-invigorates-political-activism-and-tackles-apathy/.

Lee, Jong-Wha and Warwick J. McKibbin. 2012. "The Impact of SARS." In *China: New Engine of World Growth*, edited by Ross Garnaut and Ligang Song, 19–33. Canberra: ANU Press.

Li Yang Hsu and Min-Han Tan. 2020. "What Singapore Can Teach the U.S. about Responding to Covid-19." *Stat*, 23 March, https://www.statnews.com/2020/03/23/singapore-teach-united-states-about-covid-19-response/.

Lieberman, Evan S. 2009. *Boundaries of Contagion: How Ethnic Politics Have Shaped Government Responses to AIDS*. Princeton: Princeton University Press.

Liew Chin Tong. 2020a. "Muhyiddin's Post-Covid-19 Dilemma." April 20, https://www.liewchintong.com/2020/04/20/muhyiddins-post-covid-19-dilemma/ (accessed July 18, 2020).

———. 2020b. "No Better Time for Time For a Healthier Distribution of Power to the States." May 4, https://www.liewchintong.com/2020/05/04/no-better-time-for-a-healthier-distribution-of-power-to-the-states/ (accessed July 28, 2020).

Lim, Linda. 2020. "COVID-19's Implications for Singapore's Future Economy." *Academia.SG*, April 13, https://www.academia.sg/academic-views/covid-19s-implications-for-singapores-future-economy/.

Lindsey, Tim and Max Walden. 2021. "Indonesia May Be on the Cusp of a Major COVID Spike. Unlike Its Neighbours, Though, There Is No Lockdown Yet." *The Conversation*, June 2, https://theconversation.com/indonesia-may-be-on-the-cusp-of-a-major-covid-spike-unlike-its-neighbours-though-there-is-no-lockdown-yet-158955.

Lopes, Marina. 2021. "Not Even Singapore's Rules Could Keep the Coronavirus at Bay." *Washington Post*, May 21, https://www.washingtonpost.com/world/asia_pacific/covid-singapore-lockdown-virus/2021/05/21/8870ca20-b6f5-11eb-bc4a-62849cf6cca9_story.html.

Lu, Mu. 2020. "Nation's Accountability System Effective Amid Virus Battle." *Global Times*, March 9, https://www.globaltimes.cn/content/1182074.shtml.

Lumanauw, Novy, Lenny Tristia Tambun, and Yustinus Paat 2020. "Jokowi Declares "New Normal" with Help from Military and Police." *Jakarta Globe*, May 26, https://jakartaglobe.id/news/jokowi-declares-new-normal-with-help-from-military-and-police.

Mahtani, Shibani. 2020. "Singapore Introduced Tough Laws Against Fake News. Coronavirus Has Put Them to the Test." *Washington Post*, March 16, https://www.washingtonpost.com/world/asia_pacific/exploiting-fake-news-laws-singapore-targets-tech-firms-over-coronavirus-falsehoods/2020/03/16/a49d6aa0-5f8f-11ea-ac50-18701e14e06d_story.html.

Makabenta, Yen. 2020. "The World's Longest Lockdown, Oddest Task Force vs Covid-19." *Manila Times*, May 21, https://www.manilatimes.net/2020/05/21/opinion/columnists/topanalysis/the-worlds-longest-lockdown-oddest-task-force-vs-covid-19/726169/.

Malaysiakini. 2020a. "Establish Sentencing Guidelines to Prevent Disparity When Enforcing MCO – Lawyers Group." *Malaysiakini*, April 1, https://www.malaysiakini.com/news/518147.

2020b. "Harapan MPs Claim Perikatan Hijacking Food Aid." *Malaysiakini*, April 9, https://www.malaysiakini.com/news/519753.

2020c. "Will Food Aid in Johor Be Distributed via Perikatan Leaders, JB MP Asks." *Malaysiakini*, April 23, https://www.malaysiakini.com/news/522183.

Matus, Kira, Naubahar Sharif, Alvin Li, et al. 2023. "From SARS to COVID-19: The Role of Experience and Experts in Hong Kong's Initial Policy Response to an Emerging Pandemic." *Humanities and Social Sciences Communications* 10: article 9.

McCarthy, John and Mulyadi Sumarto. 2018. "Distributional Politics and Social Protection in Indonesia: Dilemma of Layering, Nesting and Social Fit in Jokowi's Poverty Policy." *Journal of Southeast Asian Economies* 35(2): 223–236.

McDonald, Timothy. 2021. "Singapore Has COVID-19 Well under Control – But Its Migrant Workers Still Face Year-old Restrictions." *Fortune*, April 7, https://fortune.com/2021/04/07/singapore-covid-migrant-workers-restrictions-dormitories/.

McDonnell, Erin Metz. 2020. *Patchwork Leviathan: Pockets of Bureaucratic Effectiveness in Developing States*. Princeton: Princeton University Press.

McGuire, James W. 2020. *Democracy and Population Health*. Cambridge: Cambridge University Press.

McQuay, Kim, Mandakini Devasher Surie, and Nicola Nixon. 2020. "Covid Lays Bare The Flaws in Asia's Booming Megacities." *InAsia* blog, August 19, https://asiafoundation.org/2020/08/19/covid-lays-bare-the-flaws-in-asias-booming-megacities/.

Meagher, Dominic. 2020. "What's the Secret to Southeast Asia's Covid Success Stories?" *The Interpreter*, Lowy Institute, July 28, https://www.lowyinstitute.org/the-interpreter/what-s-secret-southeast-asia-covid-success-stories.

Meckelburg, Rebecca. 2020. "From the Field: COVID-19 Responses in Central Java." *New Mandala*, April 17, https://www.newmandala.org/from-the-field-covid-19-responses-in-central-java/.

Menon, Jayant. 2020. "COVID-19 and ASEAN+3: Impacts and Responses." Perspective No. 54, Singapore: ISEAS–Yusof Ishak Institute.

Mietzner, Marcus. 2015. "Reinventing Asian Populism Jokowi's Rise, Democracy, and Political Contestation in Indonesia." Policy Studies No. 72. Honolulu: East-West Center.

2020. "Populist Anti-Scientism, Religious Polarisation, and Institutionalised Corruption: How Indonesia's Democratic Decline Shaped Its COVID-19 Response." *Journal of Current Southeast Asian Affairs* 39(2): 227–249.

2021. *Democratic Deconsolidation in Southeast Asia*. New York: Cambridge University Press.

Mohd Farhaan, Shah. 2020. "Umno VP: The Era of the Federal Govt Calling the Shots Is Over." *The Star*, May 4, https://www.thestar.com.my/news/nation/2020/05/04/umno-vp-the-era-of-the-federal-govt-calling-the-shots-is-over.

Mudassir, Rayful. 2020. "55 Daerah Belum Lapor Penggunaan Anggaran Covid-19 ke Kemendagri." *Bisnis Indonesia*, June 15, https://kabar24.bisnis.com/read/20200615/15/1252905/55-daerah-belum-lapor-penggunaan-anggaran-covid-19-ke-kemendagri.

Murphy, John. 2019. "The Historical Development of Indonesian Social Security." *Asian Journal of Social Science* 47: 255–279.

Negara, Siwage Dharma and Francis E. Hutchinson. 2021. "The Impact of Indonesia's Decentralization Reforms Two Decades On: Introduction." *Journal of Southeast Asian Economies* 38(3): 289–295.

Neo, Jaclyn and Darius Lee. 2020. "Singapore's Legislative Approach to the COVID-19 Public Health 'Emergency.'" *VerfBlog*, April 18, https://verfassungsblog.de/singapores-legislative-approach-to-the-covid-19-public-health-emergency/.

Ngu Ik Tien. 2021. "The Politics of Food Aid in Sarawak, Malaysia." *Contemporary Southeast Asia* 43(1): 83–89.

Nguyen, Hong Kong and Tung Manh Ho. 2020. "Vietnam's COVID-19 Strategy: Mobilizing Public Compliance Via Accurate and Credible Communications." Perspective No. 69, Singapore: ISEAS–Yusof Ishak Institute.

Nguyen, Tran. 2020. "COVID-19 – What Do We Know about the Situation in Vietnam?" *Towards Data Science*, May 2, https://towardsdatascience.com/covid-19-what-do-we-know-about-the-situation-in-vietnam-82c195163d7e.

Nguyen, Trang and Edmund Malesky. 2020. "Reopening Vietnam: How the Country's Improving Governance Helped It Weather the COVID-19 Pandemic." *Order from Chaos* blog, Brookings, May 20, https://www.brookings.edu/blog/order-from-chaos/2020/05/20/reopening-vietnam-how-the-countrys-improving-governance-helped-it-weather-the-covid-19-pandemic/.

NST. 2020. "PM's Full Speech on Prihatin Economic Stimulus Package." *New Straits Times*, March 28, https://www.nst.com.my/news/nation/2020/03/578956/pms-full-speech-prihatin-economic-stimulus-package.

OCCRP. 2020. "Philippines Offers $600 for Information on Corrupt Officials." Organized Crime and Corruption Reporting Project, May 7, https://www.occrp.org/en/news/philippines-offers-600-for-information-on-corrupt-officials.

Olivia, Susan, John Gibson, and Rus'an Nasrudin. 2020. "A Survey of Recent Developments: Indonesia in the Time of COVID-19." *Bulletin of Indonesian Economic Studies* 56(2): 143–174.

Ooi Kok Hin. 2020. "'Call Me Abah': The Politics of Infantile Paternalism." *Naratif Malaysia*, October 7, https://naratifmalaysia.wordpress.com/2020/10/07/call-me-abah-the-politics-of-infantile-paternalism/.

Ostwald, Kai, Yuhki Tajima, and Krislert Samphantharak. 2016. "Indonesia's Decentralization Experiment: Motivations, Successes, and Unintended Consequences." *Southeast Asian Economies* 33(2): 139–156.

Paddock, Richard C. 2020. "In Indonesia, False Virus Cures Pushed by Those Who Should Know Better." *New York Times*, July 31, https://www.nytimes.com/2020/07/31/world/asia/indonesia-coronavirus.html.

Pajai, Wanpen. 2021. "As Virus Hits, Bangkok Undergoes Reverse Migration Flow." *Southeast Asia Globe*, June 8, https://southeastasiaglobe.com/thailand-migration-covid/.

Panda, Bhuputra and Harshad P. Thakur. 2016. "Decentralization and Health System Performance – A Focused Review of Dimensions, Difficulties, and Derivatives in India." *BMC Health Services Research* 16(Suppl. 6): 1–14.

Pangestika, Dyaning. 2020. "'We Don't Want People to Panic': Jokowi Says on Lack of Transparency About COVID Cases." *Jakarta Post*, March 14, https://www.thejakartapost.com/news/2020/03/13/we-dont-want-people-to-panic-jokowi-says-on-lack-of-transparency-about-covid-cases.html.

Peter, Zsombor. 2021. "Myanmar's Efforts to Control COVID-19 Crumble since February Coup, Aid Groups Say." *VOA News*, April 12, https://www.voanews.com/a/east-asia-pacific_myanmars-efforts-control-covid-19-crumble-february-coup-aid-groups-say/6204461.html.

Petersen, German. 2020. "Democracy, Authoritarianism, and COVID-19 Pandemic Management: The Case of SARS-CoV-2 Testing." Working Paper, July 15, https://www.researchgate.net/publication/342771835_Democracy_Authoritarianism_and_COVID-19_Pandemic_Management_The_Case_of_SARS-CoV-2_Testing.

Piyapong Boossabong and Pobsook Chamchong. 2020. "Coping with COVID-19 in a Non-democratic System: Policy Lessons from Thailand's Centralised Government." *International Review of Public Policy* 2(3): 358–371.

Plan International. 2021. "Smart, Successful, Strong: The Case for Investing in Adolescent Girls' Education in Aid and COVID-19 Response and

Recovery." March 16, https://www.plan.org.au/publications/smart-successful-strong/.
Porcalla, Delon. 2014. "Task Force on Emerging Infectious Diseases Formed." *Philippine Star*, June 3, https://www.philstar.com/headlines/2014/06/03/1330458/task-force-emerging-infectious-diseases-formed.
Power, Thomas and Eve Warburton, eds. 2020. *Democracy in Indonesia: From Stagnation to Regression?* Singapore: Institute of Southeast Asian Studies.
Pramita, Dini, Agung Sedayu, and Erwan Hermawan. 2020. "Bolong-bolong BPJS." *Majalah Tempo*, June 6, https://majalah.tempo.co/read/investigasi/160658/investigasi-penyebab-sebenarnya-bpjs-kesehatan-selalu-defisit.
Quach, Ha-Linh and Ngoc-Anh Hoang. 2020. "COVID-19 in Vietnam: A Lesson of Pre-preparation." *Journal of Clinical Virology* 127, https://doi.org/10.1016/j.jcv.2020.104379.
Rahma, Andita. 2020. "KPK Temukan Empat Titik Rawan Korupsi Bansos Covid-19." *Tempo*, May 20, https://nasional.tempo.co/read/1344286/kpk-temukan-empat-titik-rawan-korupsi-bansos-covid-19#.
Rahman, Dzulfiqar Fathur. 2020. "Governor Anies Calls for Greater Authority to Handle COVID-19 Epicenter." *Jakarta Post*, April 2, https://www.thejakartapost.com/news/2020/04/02/governor-anies-calls-for-greater-authority-to-handle-covid-19-epicenter.html.
Rahman, Serina. 2021. "Malaysia's Nationwide MCO – Denial, Doubts and Divisions Threaten Effectiveness." *CNA*, May 12, https://www.channelnewsasia.com/commentary/malaysia-mco-rules-activities-covid-19-coronavirus-division-1361191.
Rahmat Khairulrijal. 2020. "7,500 Military Personnel Enforcing MCO Nationwide." *New Straits Times*, March 22, https://www.nst.com.my/news/nation/2020/03/577213/7500-military-personnel-enforcing-mco-nationwide.
Reed, John. 2020. "Ayala Wins over Duterte with Rapid Response to Covid-19." *Financial Times*, July 5, https://www.ft.com/content/a6919b0a-b95e-4e9a-bf82-69357abaf9ff.
Rochmyaningsih, Dyna. 2020. "Indonesian Health Minister under Fire for Pushing His Own Controversial Stroke Treatment." *Science*, January 10, https://www.sciencemag.org/news/2020/01/indonesian-health-minister-under-fire-pushing-his-own-controversial-stroke-treatment.
Rodzi, Nadirah H. 2020. "Malaysian Govt Accused of Double Standards on Social Distancing Rules." *Straits Times*, April 21, https://www.straitstimes.com/asia/se-asia/malaysian-govt-accused-of-double-standards-on-social-distancing-rules.

Romero, Egundo Eclar. 2020. "Design Thinking." *Philippine Daily Inquirer*, May 4, https://opinion.inquirer.net/129474/design-thinking#ixzz6RTZaflaa.

Rood, Steven. 2019. "Finding Federalism in the Philippines: Federalism – 'The centrepiece of my campaign.'" In *From Aquino II to Duterte (2010–2018): Change, Continuity – and Rupture*, edited by Imelda Deinla and Björn Dressel, 62–98. Singapore: ISEAS Publishing.

Rosser, Andrew. 2012. "Realising Free Health Care for the Poor in Indonesia: The Politics of Illegal Fees." *Journal of Contemporary Asia* 42(2): 255–275.

Rosser, Andrew and John Murphy. 2023. *Contesting Social Welfare in Southeast Asia*. Cambridge: Cambridge University Press.

Rosser, Andrew and Ian Wilson. 2012. "Democratic Decentralisation and Pro-Poor Policy Reform in Indonesia: The Politics of Health Insurance for the Poor in Jembrana and Tabanan." *Asian Journal of Social Science* 40 (5–6): 608–634.

Routley, Laura. 2012. "Developmental States: A Review of the Literature." ESID Working Paper No. 03. Manchester: Effective States and Inclusive Development Research Centre.

Sachs, Jeffrey D. 2021. "Reasons for Asia-Pacific Success in Suppressing COVID-19." *World Happiness Report*, March 20, https://worldhappiness.report/ed/2021/reasons-for-asia-pacific-success-in-suppressing-covid-19/.

Sambhi, Natalie. 2021. "Generals Gaining Ground: Civil-Military Relations and Democracy in Indonesia." Brookings Institution, January 22, https://www.brookings.edu/articles/generals-gaining-ground-civil-military-relations-and-democracy-in-indonesia/.

Santos, Ana P. 2021. "COVID: Police Harassment Threatens Philippine Food Pantries." DW, April 27, https://www.dw.com/en/covid-police-harassment-threatens-grassroots-community-pantries-in-the-philippines/a-57350186.

Sari, Lila, Edward Aspinall, Haryanto, and Andi Adli Armunanto, 2023, "Parties, Patronage and COVID-19 Vaccination Distribution in Indonesia." *Contemporary Southeast Asia* 45(1): 1–29.

Searight, Amy. 2020. "Strengths and Vulnerabilities in Southeast Asia's Response to the Covid-19 Pandemic." CSIS, April 20, https://www.csis.org/analysis/strengths-and-vulnerabilities-southeast-asias-response-covid-19-pandemic.

See, Aie Balagtas. 2021. "Rodrigo Duterte Is Using One of the World's Longest COVID-19 Lockdowns to Strengthen His Grip on the Philippines." *Time*, March 15, https://time.com/5945616/covid-philippines-pandemic-lockdown/.

Shad Saleem Faruqi. 2020. "State Defiance Lacks Legal Basis." *The Star*, 7 May, https://www.thestar.com.my/opinion/columnists/reflecting-on-the-law/2020/05/07/state-defiance-lacks-legal-basis.

Shalilah, Nur Fitriatus. 2020. "Harga Tes Covid-19 Mahal, Ini Kata Kemenkes dan YLKI." *Kompas*, June 21, https://www.kompas.com/tren/read/2020/06/21/070800965/harga-tes-covid-19-mahal-ini-kata-kemenkes-dan-ylki?page=all.

Singh, Prerna. 2024. "The Politics of Contagion: States, Societies, and the Control and Consequences of Infectious Diseases." *Annual Review of Political Science* 27: 355–380.

Siregar, Rizki Nauli, Rus'an Nasrudin, Gumilang Aryo Sahadewo, et al. 2020. *Hasil Survei terhadap Ekonomi terkait Kebijakan Saat Krisis Covid-19*. Jakarta: Indonesian Regional Science Association, https://irsa.or.id/wp-content/uploads/2020/04/Survei_Covid-19.pdf.

Sirisak Laochankham, Peerasit Kamnuansilpa, and Grichawat Lowatcharin. 2021. "Locally Driven Action in Pandemic Control: The Case of Khon Kaen Province, Thailand." *Contemporary Southeast Asia* 43(1): 8–14.

Slater, Dan. 2018. "Party Cartelization, Indonesian-style: Presidential Power-sharing and the Contingency of Democratic Opposition." *Journal of East Asian Studies* 18(1): 23–46.

Sochua, Mo. 2020. "Coronavirus 'Fake News' Arrests Are Quieting Critics." *Foreign Policy*, May 22, https://foreignpolicy.com/2020/05/22/coronavirus-fake-news-arrests-quiet-critics-southeast-asia/.

Sukhani, Piya. 2020. "The Domesticated Doraemon: The Outlook for Women under Perikatan Nasional." *New Mandala*, June 10, https://www.newmandala.org/the-domesticated-doraemon-the-outlook-for-women-under-perikatan-nasional/.

Sukumaran, Tashny and Bhavan Jaipragas. 2020. "Coronavirus: Hundreds Arrested as Malaysia Cracks Down on Migrants in Covid-19 Red Zones." *South China Morning Post*, May 1, https://www.scmp.com/week-asia/politics/article/3082529/coronavirus-hundreds-arrested-malaysia-cracks-down-migrants.

Supalak Ganjaakhundee. 2020. *COVID-19 in Thailand: The Securitization of a Non-traditional Threat*. Perspective No. 51. Singapore: ISEAS–Yusuf Ishak Institute.

Suzuki, Ayame. 2020. "Philippines Response to COVID-19: Limits of State Capacity." *CSEAS Corona Chronicles*, June 23, https://covid-19chronicles.cseas.kyoto-u.ac.jp/post-046-html/.

SWS. 2020. "SWS May 4–10, 2020 Covid-19 Mobile Phone Survey – Report No. 12: Record-high 43% of Filipinos Expect Their Life to Worsen in the

Next 12 Months." Social Weather Stations, June 23, https://www.sws.org.ph/swsmain/artcldisppage/?artcsyscode=ART-20200623103236.

Sy, Peter A. 2003. "Welfarism versus Free Enterprise: Considerations of Power and Justice in the Philippine Healthcare System." *Bioethics* 17(5–6): 555–566.

Syakriah, Ardila. 2020. "COVID-19: Anies Slams Health Ministry's Requirements for Large-Scale Social Restrictions." *Jakarta Post*, April 5, https://www.thejakartapost.com/news/2020/04/05/covid-19-anies-slams-health-ministrys-requirements-for-large-scale-social-restrictions.html.

Tan, Hsien-Li. 2020. "A Collective ASEAN Response to COVID-19." *East Asia Forum*, 16 July, https://www.eastasiaforum.org/2020/07/16/a-collective-asean-response-to-covid-19/.

Tan, Kenneth Paul. 2018. *Singapore: Identity, Brand, Power*. Cambridge: Cambridge University Press.

Tan, Yvette. 2020. "Covid-19 Singapore: A 'Pandemic of Inequality' Exposed." *BBC News*, September 18, https://www.bbc.com/news/world-asia-54082861.

Tempo. 2024. "Rencana Usang Menghapus Pilkada Langsung." *Tempo*, December 18, https://www.tempo.co/kolom/bahaya-pilkada-oleh-dprd-1182973.

Teo You Yenn and Ng Kok How. 2020. "Crisis is Exactly the Time to Make Structural Changes to Address Poverty and Inequality." *Academia.SG*, March 17, https://www.academia.sg/academic-views/crisis-is-exactly-the-time-to-make-structural-changes-to-address-poverty-and-inequality/.

Termsak Chalermpalanupap. 2020. "COVID-19: Prayut's Dilemma – Save Lives or Jobs." Perspective No. 38. Singapore: ISEAS–Yusof Ishak Institute.

Thanthong-Knight, Randy. 2021. "Thai Protesters Plan Return to Streets as COVID-19 Response Fuels Disquiet." May 21, https://www.japantimes.co.jp/news/2021/05/21/asia-pacific/thai-protests-comeback/.

Thompson, Mark R. 2001. "Whatever Happened to 'Asian Values'?" *Journal of Democracy* 12(4): 154–165.

Thoreson, Ryan. 2020. "Philippines Uses Humiliation as COVID-19 Curfew Punishment." Human Rights Watch, April 8. https://perma.cc/X3PJ-9PTX

Tiberghien, Yves. 2021. *The East Asian COVID-19 Paradox*. Cambridge: Cambridge University Press.

Today. 2020. "New Dorms with 'Better Standards' to Be Built for 100,000 Foreign Workers in Coming Years: Lawrence Wong." *Today*, June 1, https://www.todayonline.com/singapore/new-dorms-better-standards-be-built-100000-foreign-workers-coming-years-lawrence-wong.

Toh Ee Ming. 2020. "Pushed Down a Rung." *Southeast Asia Globe*, April 8, https://southeastasiaglobe.com/singapore-urban-poor-covid/.

Tomacruz, Sofia. 2020. "'Shoot Them Dead': Duterte Orders Troops to Kill Quarantine Violators." *Rappler*, April 1, https://www.rappler.com/philippines/256705-duterte-orders-troops-shoot-kill-coronavirus-quarantine-violators/.

Tomsa, Dirk. 2015. "Toning Down the 'Big Bang': The Politics of Decentralisation during the Yudhoyono Years." In *The Yudhoyono Presidency: Indonesia's Decade of Stability and Stagnation*, edited by Edward Aspinall, Marcus Mietzner, and Dirk Tomsa, 155–174. Singapore: ISEAS–Yusof Ishak Institute.

UNODC. [2020]. "Covid-19 Emergency Packages in Southeast Asia." United Nations Office on Drugs and Crime, Regional Office for Southeast Asia and the Pacific, https://www.unodc.org/roseap/en/what-we-do/anti-corruption/topics/covid-19.html.

Venzon, Cliff. 2020. "Duterte Apologises to Philippine Tycoons He Threatened to Send to Jail." *Nikkei Asian Review*, May 5, https://asia.nikkei.com/Business/Companies/Duterte-apologizes-to-Philippine-tycoons-he-threatened-to-jail.

Vu Thanh Tu Anh. 2016. "Vietnam: Decentralization Amidst Fragmentation." *Journal of Southeast Asian Economies* 33(2): 188–208.

Warburton, Eve. 2016. "Jokowi and the New Developmentalism." *Bulletin of Indonesian Economic Studies* 53(2): 297–320.

Washida, Hidekuni. 2019. *Distributive Politics in Malaysia: Maintaining Authoritarian Party Dominance*. New York: Routledge.

Weiss, Meredith L. 2020. *The Roots of Resilience: Party Machines and Grassroots Politics in Southeast Asia*. Ithaca, NY: Cornell University Press.

Weiss, Meredith L., Paul Hutchcroft, Allen Hicken, and Edward Aspinall. 2021. "One War, Many Battles: COVID-19 in Urban Southeast Asia." *Contemporary Southeast Asia* 43(1): 1–7.

Wenham, Clare. 2018. "Regionalizing Health Security: Thailand's Leadership Ambitions in Mainland Southeast Asian Disease Control." *Contemporary Southeast Asia* 40(1): 126–151.

Wenham, Clare, Joshua W. Busby, Jeremy Youde, and Asha Herten-Crabb. 2023. "From Imperialism to the 'Golden Age' to the Great Lockdown: The Politics of Global Health Governance." *Annual Review of Political Science* 26(1): 431–450.

Willoughby, Emma. 2021. "Unified, Preventive, Low-Cost Government Response to COVID-19 in Việt Nam." In *Coronavirus Politics: The Comparative Politics and Policy of COVID-19*, edited by Scott L. Greer, Elizabeth J. King, Elize Massard da Fonseca, and Andre Peralta-Santos, 127–145. Ann Arbor: University of Michigan Press.

Wong Chin-Huat. 2020. "Malaysia: Coronavirus, Political Coup and Lockdown." *The Round Table*, 109(3): 337–337.

Wong, Joseph. 2004. *Healthy Democracies: Welfare Politics in Taiwan and South Korea.* Ithaca, NY: Cornell University Press.

―― 2025. *The Welfare State in East Asia.* Cambridge: Cambridge University Press.

Wong, Lawrence. 2020. "Remarks at Press Conference on COVID-19, National Press Centre." April 9, https://www.sgpc.gov.sg/sgpcmedia/media_releases/mnd/speech/S-20200409-1/attachment/Remarks%20by%20Minister%20Lawrence%20Wong%20at%209%20Apr%20Press%20Conference%20on%20COVID-19%20final.pdf (accessed July 25, 2020).

World Bank. 2021a. *East Asia and Pacific Economic Update, April 2021: Uneven Recovery.* Washington, DC: World Bank.

―― 2021b. *Philippines Economic Update, June 2021: Navigating a Challenging Recovery.* Washington, DC: World Bank.

Yee, Jovic, and Aurelio, Julie M. 2020. "High Number of Virus-Hit Health Workers Makes PH 'an Outlier.'" *Philippine Daily Inquirer*, April 22, https://newsinfo.inquirer.net/1262625/high-number-of-virus-hit-health-workers-makes-ph-an-outlier#ixzz8jGEdabpQ.

Yeoh Lam Keong, Manu Bhaskaran, Donald Low, and Tan Kim Song. 2020. "Supporting Small Businesses and the Poor in this Pandemic." *Academia.SG*, April 28, https://www.academia.sg/coronavirus/smes-and-the-poor/.

Yeoh, Tricia. 2019. "Reviving the Spirit of Federalism: Decentralisation Policy Options for a New Malaysia." Policy Ideas No. 59. Kuala Lumpur: Institute for Democracy and Economic Affairs.

―― 2020. "Infusing Federalism into Public Health Decision-making." *Malaysiakini*, May 4, https://malaysiakini.com/news/524123.

Yuda, Tauchid Komara, and Stefan Kühner. 2023. "Bringing Indonesia into the Global Welfare Regime Debate: A Literature Review and Future Research Agenda." *Asian Social Work and Policy Review* 17(2): 103–114.

Zhacky, Mochamad. 2020. Polri Tetapkan 51 Tersangka Penyebar Hoax Terkait Virus Corona," *Detiknews*, March 31, https://news.detik.com/berita/d-4959495/polri-tetapkan-51-tersangka-penyebar-hoax-terkait-virus-corona.

Acknowledgements

My deep appreciation to Edward Aspinall and Nicole Curato for their collaboration on previous versions of this volume and subsequent feedback. Not only would the work be weaker without their contributions – some of which remain incorporated into the text, with their permission – but it would not have been written at all. Sincere thanks also to Wei-Ting Yen and the press's reviewers for their exceptionally constructive critiques and suggestions, and to Lucy Rhymer for stepping in as series editor for this volume.

Politics and Society in Southeast Asia

Edward Aspinall
Australian National University

Edward Aspinall is a professor of politics at the Coral Bell School of Asia-Pacific Affairs, Australian National University. A specialist of Southeast Asia, especially Indonesia, much of his research has focused on democratisation, ethnic politics and civil society in Indonesia and, most recently, clientelism across Southeast Asia.

Meredith L. Weiss
University at Albany, SUNY

Meredith L. Weiss is Professor of Political Science at the University at Albany, SUNY. Her research addresses political mobilization and contention, the politics of identity and development, and electoral politics in Southeast Asia, with particular focus on Malaysia and Singapore.

About the Series

The Elements series Politics and Society in Southeast Asia includes both country-specific and thematic studies on one of the world's most dynamic regions. Each title, written by a leading scholar of that country or theme, combines a succinct, comprehensive, up-to-date overview of debates in the scholarly literature with original analysis and a clear argument.

Cambridge Elements

Politics and Society in Southeast Asia

Elements in the Series

Organized Labor in Southeast Asia
Teri L. Caraway

The Philippines: From 'People Power' to Democratic Backsliding
Mark R. Thompson

Contesting Social Welfare in Southeast Asia
Andrew Rosser and John Murphy

The Politics of Cross-Border Mobility in Southeast Asia
Michele Ford

Myanmar: A Political Lexicon
Nick Cheesman

Courts and Politics in Southeast Asia
Björn Dressel

Thailand: Contestation, Polarization, and Democratic Regression
Prajak Kongkirati

Social Media and Politics in Southeast Asia
Merlyna Lim

State and Sub-State Nationalism in Southeast Asia
Jacques Bertrand

Rethinking Colonial Legacies across Southeast Asia: Through the Lens of the Japanese Wartime Empire
Diana S. Kim

Sustainable Development and the Environment in Southeast Asia
Pamela D. McElwee

Politics in a Pandemic: Governance and Crisis Management in Southeast Asia
Meredith L. Weiss

A full series listing is available at: www.cambridge.org/ESEA

For EU product safety concerns, contact us at Calle de José Abascal, 56–1°,
28003 Madrid, Spain or eugpsr@cambridge.org.

www.ingramcontent.com/pod-product-compliance
Lightning Source LLC
LaVergne TN
LVHW011849060526
838200LV00054B/4253